get cooking

Sam Stern

and Susan Stern, who got him started

CANDLEWICK PRESS

contents

WELCOME TO MY THIRD BOOK!

How did it come about? I love a challenge. So when seven friends asked me to sort out some top-tasting recipes based on their one favorite food, I went for it.

It wasn't easy. Particularly as some of them went for whole food groups (thanks, guys) instead of single ingredients. But no problem. I just got into the kitchen and got creative. You'll see the book's got eight chapters—one for each mate and their ingredient of choice. That's tomatoes from Jess, cheese from Henry, pasta from Ariyo, vegetables from Joe, meat from Andy, potatoes from Liv, and sweet stuff from Verity. I kept the best for myself—chocolate. You'll meet all my mates later.

Why cook?

Hey, you're missing out if you don't do it. Every part of the process has something cool going for it. First off—the shopping. Nope, food doesn't grow in bags. Food shopping means you get to visit some great markets, shops, delis, farm stands—even the supermarket. Do it. Get out there. Talk to the people who've grown the stuff or made it. You want to know where your food has come from and how it's been produced. Keep it real. You want it to be good if you're going to swallow it.

Cooking gives you power in loads of ways. It's a great way to be independent— chucking some good stuff together when you're just in or before you go out. Getting yourself ready for when you escape from home to work, college, travel, or whatever. Cooking the right stuff can wake you up (after a night out), sort you out (when you're feeling lousy or exams loom), cheer you up (head straight for chocolate), or give you the energy you need just to get through the day, the party, the game, or another night of practice. Then there's the ultimate pleasure of cooking itself. The hands-on and senses stuff—melting chocolate, separating an egg, kneading dough, curing salmon, or making puffy Yorkshire puddings; putting together a whole roast dinner; watching a mess of mix be transformed into something magnificent and appetizing.

Cooking gets you into politics, too. Recently, there's been loads of debate about food—organic vs. nonorganic; fast food vs. slower food (no contest); growing your own food (do it—in tires, flower gardens, window boxes, and even windowsills); and food miles (read labels—get local if you can, as it should be fresher and better, but check it out). Cooking's the key to everything. It takes you beyond the plate to a great way of living.

Finally, the best bit: feeding other people at everyday meals, parties, and gatherings. It's all about good times. Everyone helping out in the kitchen, then sitting around eating together and having a good laugh. Cooking for your friends and family is the greatest pleasure (as well as impressive!). So over to you.

Enjoy, and get cooking!

Tomatoes

Jess has great taste and likes to take good care of herself, so it's no surprise she went for tomatoes. They're healthy. (Who needs make-up? Tomatoes help out your eyes, skin, and immune system.) They're stylish, versatile, and perfect to photograph. Slice 'em up with shallots or herbs and a sharp dressing, or cook 'em up for my salsa, bakes, soup, or homestyle ketchup. Support the main event in awesome meat dishes (lush tomato sauce with tuna and mash or my-style chicken parmigiana). Use them sun-dried in a marvelous burger. Skin and chop 'em small for an impressive retro cocktail. These guys look and taste good enough for an exhibition. Blitz 'em raw for dipping dough balls in. Winter tomatoes can be inferior. OK, they look cool, but it's all skin-deep. Use canned for a great Margherita-style tart and deeply flavored sauces. Buying fresh? Sniff. They should smell peppery. Grow cherry tomatoes on your windowsill (late July to August). Larger varieties work in a flower bed, growbag, camera bag, handbag. . . .

Tomato, Squash, & Prosciutto Salad

Serves 4
Ingredients
1 butternut squash
Olive oil for roasting
Sprinkle of crushed chili
  flakes
½ teaspoon ground cumin
Sea salt and pepper
1 ciabatta or focaccia
  loaf, cubed
8 to12 slices prosciutto or
  ham
16 to 20 cherry tomatoes
  (some red, some yellow's
  nice)
Arugula or spinach leaves
Parmesan shavings or curls
Olive oil and balsamic
  vinegar for drizzling

Variation
VEGGIE
Substitute ham and
Parmesan with chunks
of smoked cheese,
avocado, and sliced red
onion.

This is nice. Cherry tomatoes create bursts of flavor that work brilliantly with the other tastes and textures. Be artistic with your assembly. Missing an ingredient? Experiment with substitutes.

Directions
1. Preheat oven to 400°F.
2. **Squash:** Wash and dry. Slice the ends off. Hold firmly and cut in two lengthwise down the center. Remove seeds with a spoon. Discard.
3. Cut the squash (peel on) into bite-size bits. Slap on an oiled roasting pan or baking sheet. Drizzle and coat with olive oil. Sprinkle with chili, cumin, sea salt, and pepper to taste. Bake for at least 20 minutes till soft and just browning (could take longer).
4. **Croutons:** While the squash cooks, roll the bread cubes in a bit of oil and salt. Cook on a baking sheet for 5 minutes or more, till crisp and golden.
5. **Assemble:** Drape the ham over plates. Slap the squash on top with the cherry tomatoes and arugula or spinach. Scatter the croutons and curls or shavings of Parmesan over the lot. Drizzle with a bit of olive oil and/or balsamic or your favorite dressing.

Dough Balls & Tomato-Chili Salsa

Dunk your own dough balls into this brilliant tomato-chili salsa for a popular spicy hit. Stuffed or plain, they're perfect for parties. Knock out a few the next time you're making pizza.

Directions

1. Dough: Make pizza dough (page 34), but at STEP 1, add the garlic and rosemary. Follow the recipe until the end of STEP 3.

2. Preheat oven to 425°F. Lightly grease 2 baking sheets.

3. Slap the risen dough onto a lightly floured board. Knead for 2 minutes.

4. Plain balls: Break bits off. Roll into smooth, neat walnut-size balls.

Stuffed balls: Shape each bit into a smooth, flat circle. Stick an olive or cheese chunk in the middle. Draw the dough up and around to cover it. Pinch the ends firmly together. A bit of water may help to seal.

5. Set the balls apart on the baking sheets, seams down. Brush with the milk or beaten egg. Bake for 15 minutes or till cooked and golden. Split a bit? No problem!

6. Salsa: Chuck the ingredients in a blender or processor. Blitz till smooth. Strain into a pan. Heat gently (don't boil). Taste and adjust seasoning.

7. Dunk hot (or cold) balls into warm salsa.

Makes 20 to 30 balls

Ingredients
Pizza dough (page 34)
3 cloves garlic, finely chopped
1 to 2 sprigs of rosemary, finely chopped
Beaten egg or milk for brushing

Fillings
Pitted olives
Mozzarella, cubed

Salsa
2½ cups chopped tomatoes
1 small onion, peeled and halved
2 cloves garlic, peeled
2 red chili peppers, de-seeded and finely chopped
1 teaspoon sugar
Salt and black pepper
Juice of 1 lime
2 tablespoons olive oil

Why Not?

Dunk into:
Salsa verde (page 80)
Garlic butter (page 98)
Yogurt with dill

Tomato & Mozzarella Bruschetta

Serves 2
Ingredients
2 slices good white bread
   or focaccia
Olive oil
4 ounces (1 cup) mozzarella
2 to 3 tomatoes
1 clove garlic
1 teaspoon red wine
   vinegar or lemon juice
   (optional)
Salt and pepper (optional)

Eat with:
Spinach, lettuce, or arugula

Variations
CHEESE & HAM
Lay a slice of ham under
mozzarella before
baking.

MORE TOMATO
Rub half a whole tomato
over crisped bread at
the end of STEP 5.

I make this all the time after school or when I fancy something light but good. Bits of warm tomato lift the taste of the cheese on the crisp bread base. It may be simple, but it's pretty lovely.

Directions
1. Preheat oven to 400°F.
2. Set the bread on a baking sheet. Drizzle with a little olive oil. Bake till just crisp (5 to 10 minutes).
3. Meanwhile, thinly slice the mozzarella into ¼-inch pieces.
4. Chop the tomatoes into small cubes.
5. Remove the bread from the oven. Rub a cut clove of garlic over each slice.
6. Lay the mozzarella over the bread slices to cover. Stick bits of tomato on top with a few drops of olive oil.
7. Bake till the cheese is just softening—could be as little as 3 to 5 minutes. Remove from oven just before it melts.
8. Eat as is or slap a few more bits of tomato on top. Or toss more tomato bits in the vinegar or lemon juice, salt, and pepper, and set on the side of the plate.

Scarlet Couscous & Veggie Skewers

Liven up your couscous with tomato juice for this cool, light eat. OK, it sounds weird, but you'll get a bit of fizz and a brilliant color to set off your skewers. Perfect if you've got a few mates over or you're treating family.

Directions

1. Mix the ⅔ cup tomato juice, oil, lemon juice, 2 tablespoons water, and garlic in a large bowl.
2. Add the couscous to the liquid. Mix well. Cover with a cloth. Leave for 1 hour or longer.
3. Slap the raisins into a small bowl. Cover with boiling water and a bit of tomato juice.
4. Chop the tomatoes into small cubes (skin and de-seed if you want to—see page 14).
5. Test the couscous. Should be soft. Stir in a tablespoon of hot water if not.
6. Season with salt and pepper. Stir in the chopped tomatoes, cucumber, red pepper, onion, and herbs. Drain the raisins. Chuck them in. Pile onto a plate.
7. Thread the cherry tomatoes, onion, mushrooms, and zucchini onto metal skewers or wooden ones presoaked in cold water for 20 minutes.
8. Beat the oil and vinegar together. Drizzle over the veg.
9. Grill. Turn regularly till browned and just tender. Serve with the couscous.

Serves 3 to 4
Ingredients
⅔ cup tomato juice, plus extra
3 tablespoons olive oil
Juice of 1½ lemons
2 tablespoons boiling water, plus extra
1 clove garlic, crushed
1 cup couscous
2 tablespoons raisins
2 large or 3 medium tomatoes
Salt and pepper
6-inch piece cucumber, chopped
1 red pepper, de-seeded, chopped
1 small red onion, chopped
1 bunch parsley, chopped
1 bunch mint, chopped
Veg skewers
2 cups cherry tomatoes
1 large red onion, chopped
2 cups button mushrooms
3 cups zucchini, sliced
2 tablespoons olive oil
2 tablespoons balsamic vinegar

Eat with:
Lamb koftas (page 90)
Homestyle pork burgers (page 88)

Retro Tomato & Shrimp Cocktail

Ingredients
2 tomatoes
½ pound cooked shrimp
A little butterhead lettuce
Slice of lemon (optional)

Dressing
1 tablespoon ketchup
   (page 139)
3 tablespoons plain or
   Greek yogurt
3 tablespoons mayo
Juice of 1 lemon
1 small clove garlic, crushed
A few drops of Tabasco,
   horseradish, or wasabi
   sauce
Salt
Cayenne pepper

Eat with:
Slices of brown bread and
   butter

Variations
AVOCADO
Chop fresh avocado
into the mix and set it
on bread for an open
sandwich.

TORTILLA
Wrap it up in a
soft tortilla.

Lovely and light with a bit of a bite. Shrimp get a cool double dose of tomato. Jess piles this one high for a romantic starter. P.S. Shrimp are so good for you. . . .

Directions
1. Skinning: Stick the tomatoes into a large heatproof bowl. Pour boiling water over them. Leave for 2 minutes. Drain into a colander.
2. When cool, peel the skins off. Cut the tomatoes into quarters. Remove the seeds. Chop the remaining flesh into tiny pieces.
3. Dressing: Mix all the dressing ingredients. Taste and adjust the flavors.
4. Piling: Slap a bit of diced tomato on a plate or into the base of a short tumbler or glass. Cover with a bit of shredded lettuce.
5. Mix ⅔ of the dressing into the shrimp and the remaining diced tomato. Set this on top of the lettuce. Top with the remaining dressing, and garnish with a lemon slice, if desired.

Lovely Tomato & Garlic Soup

Roast your tomatoes for this awesome soup and you'll get the best out of them. Blasting them with heat and garlic maximizes their flavor.

Serves 4
Ingredients
2 pounds or 7 medium-
  size tomatoes
3 to 4 tablespoons olive oil
2 large onions, chopped
1 carrot, peeled and sliced
1 stick celery, sliced
1 head of garlic
2½ cups water
2 tablespoons sugar
2 tablespoons chopped
  parsley or cilantro
Salt and pepper

Eat with:
Good warm, crusty bread
Croutons (page 10)
Grated Parmesan or
  Cheddar
A whirl of sour cream

Why Not?
Add some basil leaves smashed with a bit of balsamic vinegar, salt, and sugar.

Directions
1. Preheat oven to 425°F.
2. Set the tomatoes on a baking sheet. Drizzle with a little olive oil. Roast for 20 to 25 minutes or till their skins split.
3. Meanwhile, heat 2 tablespoons of olive oil in a large pan on low heat. Slap in the onions, carrot, and celery. Cook gently for 5 to 10 minutes till soft and sweating. Stir with a wooden spoon.
4. Slice the very top off the whole garlic. Separate the cloves. Set them on the baking sheet with the roasting tomatoes. Drizzle with a bit of oil. Bake with the tomatoes for a further 10 to 15 minutes till soft. Remove.
5. Smush the garlic out of its skin. Careful—it's hot. Tip the tomatoes and garlic cloves in with the sweated vegetables. Add the water, sugar, herbs, salt, and pepper. Bring to a boil, then reduce immediately. Cover and simmer for 30 minutes.
6. Remove from heat. Cool for a bit, then, if desired, blitz in a blender till smooth. Reheat, taste, and adjust seasoning.

Chinese Ketchup Spareribs

Serves 4
Ingredients
3 pounds meaty pork
  spareribs
Marinade
3 tablespoons ketchup
  (page 139)
3 tablespoons soy sauce
3 tablespoons rice wine
½ cup hoisin sauce
2 tablespoons sugar
4 cloves garlic, crushed
Piece of fresh ginger, peeled
  and roughly grated
1 red chili pepper, de-seeded
  and sliced, or 1 tablespoon
  sweet chili sauce

Why not make up a batch of homestyle ketchup to give this great Chinese sparerib recipe a healthy kick? The concentrated tomato taste really makes the marinade. Great for dinner, a barbecue, or a Chinese-style banquet.

Directions
1. Put the ribs into a large casserole dish with water to cover.
2. Bring to a boil. Reduce heat and simmer very gently for 15 minutes. Drain in a colander and allow to cool.
3. Meanwhile, mix all the marinade ingredients together. Pour into a large shallow dish big enough to hold the ribs.
4. Put the cold ribs into the marinade. Turn them to coat. Leave for the flavors to catch for a couple of hours or even overnight.
5. Preheat oven to 350°F.
6. Lay the ribs out over a rimmed baking sheet lined with foil. Brush with the marinade. Bake for 20 minutes on each side or till tender and golden. Rest the meat somewhere warm for 5 minutes.
7. If you're making a complete meal, cook rice and make a veg stir-fry 15 minutes before you eat. Serve with soy sauce.

Smart Margherita Tart

Pretty straightforward. Pretty delicious. It's a pizza-kind of tomatoey tart. Using canned tomatoes makes it an all-year-rounder. Brilliant for parties or general sharing. Team with a bunch of lovely salads.

Directions

1. Make pastry by hand (see page 138).
2. Grease a 9-inch loose-based tart pan.
3. Roll the pastry out lightly on a floured board. Make it big enough to fit the base plus the sides of the pan.
4. Ease one edge of the pastry off the board. Roll the pin underneath to the center, then use it to lift the pastry up and over the pan. Let the pastry down onto the pan, then roll the pin away carefully. Mold the pastry gently into the pan. Fill any gaps with extra pastry. Press tears together. Chill for 30 minutes.
5. Gently heat the oil and butter in a large pan over low heat. Add the onion and garlic. Cook till soft, not colored.
6. Slap in the tomatoes, sugar, and tomato purée. Chop and add half the optional anchovies (saving the anchovy oil for later). Boil. Reduce heat. Simmer for 20 minutes. Preheat oven to 400°F.
7. Cool the mixture slightly. Add the eggs and half the herbs. Pour into tart.
8. Top with the remaining whole anchovies, olives, and herbs. Sprinkle with Parmesan and the anchovy oil from Step 6, if using.
9. Bake for 30 minutes. Reduce heat to 350°F. Cook for another 15 minutes or till crisp and cooked through.

Serves 4 to 6
Ingredients
Pastry
1 recipe short-crust pastry (page 138)
Filling
2 tablespoons olive oil
1 tablespoon butter
1 medium to large onion, chopped
3 cloves garlic, peeled and crushed
Two 14-ounce cans diced tomatoes
Pinch of sugar
2 tablespoons tomato purée
2 ounces canned anchovies, drained (optional)
3 eggs, beaten
Handful of basil or parsley, torn
Black olives
Parmesan for sprinkling

Eat with:
Green salad (page 140)
Baked potatoes (page 98)
Coleslaw (page 140)

Serves 4
Ingredients
1 pound beef for mincing (rump's good) or quality ground beef
1 small onion, peeled and finely chopped
1 clove garlic, peeled and crushed
2 ounces (1 cup) sun-dried tomatoes, chopped small
2 teaspoons ketchup (page 139)
½ tablespoon horseradish sauce or a splash of Worcestershire sauce
1 tablespoon chopped parsley
Salt and pepper
Sunflower oil
Stacking
4 burger buns
Ketchup
A little butterhead lettuce, shredded
Fresh tomatoes, thinly sliced

Celery & apple salad
2 sticks celery, thinly sliced
1 small apple, thinly sliced
2 tablespoons mayo
1 tablespoon plain or Greek yogurt
1 teaspoon Dijon mustard
Drizzle of honey
Salt and pepper

Why Not?
Dry your own tomatoes. Slice tomatoes in two. Oven dry for 8 to 10 hours at 325°F on a rack over a baking sheet. (Cherry tomatoes dry faster.) Put into jars covered with olive oil.

Tangy Tomato Burgers & Salad

Slap flavor-packing sun-dried tomatoes into these cool burgers for an awesome dish. Make lots for gatherings and parties.

Directions
To make your own ground beef, cut beef into cubes. Blitz a few at a time in the processor or mincer till it looks right. Don't overdo it.
1. Slap the ground beef into a bowl.
2. Mix all the other ingredients except oil into the beef. Fry a crumb in hot oil. Taste and adjust seasoning.
3. Shape firmly into 4 flattish burgers. If the mix is flaky, add a splash of beaten egg, ketchup, or mayo to bind it together. Chill for 30 minutes or cook right away.
4. Preheat grill, grill pan, or frying pan. Cook in oil for 3 minutes on each side (turn with care) or till done as you like. Rest the meat for 2 minutes.
5. **Salad:** Mix all the salad ingredients together in a bowl.
6. Stack the burgers as you like. Enjoy with loads of salad.

Baked Egg-Stuffed Tomatoes

A good little snack to crack into when you've got mates over for brunch or to treat yourself to anytime. Getting the eggs into the tomatoes can be a challenge, but enjoy yourself—it's worth it.

Directions

1. Slice the tops off the stem ends of the tomatoes. Using a spoon and a sharp knife, hollow them out completely. Don't break the skins.

2. Set them upside down for 10 to 20 minutes to drain. Preheat oven to 400°F.

3. Set the tomatoes on a greased baking sheet and season the insides with salt, pepper, and garlic.

4. Crack an egg over a bowl, letting a bit of white spill out. Carefully slip the rest of the egg into a tomato. Repeat for each egg.

5. Sprinkle the top with Parmesan, or make a mix of cream, tomato purée, and Parmesan. Spoon that over.

6. Bake for 15 minutes or till set as you like.

7. Serve on bits of toast or bread fried in a bit of olive oil.

Serves 2

Ingredients

4 large tomatoes
Salt and pepper
2 cloves garlic, crushed
4 medium eggs
Parmesan, freshly grated
2 tablespoons heavy cream
  or crème fraîche
  (optional)
2 teaspoons tomato purée
  (optional)
4 slices white bread
Olive oil

Eat with:

Lightly fried mushrooms
Crisp bacon

Variation

MUSHROOMS
Try with deep-cup mushrooms instead of tomatoes.

My-Style Chicken Parmigiana

Serves 4
Ingredients
4 chicken breasts
4 slices prosciutto
5-ounce ball fresh
 mozzarella or fontina
 cheese, sliced
4 fresh basil leaves
 (optional)
Salt and pepper
1 garlic clove, crushed
⅓ cup flour
2 eggs, beaten
½ cup Italian-seasoned
 breadcrumbs
Olive oil
Butter
Tomato sauce (page 21)

Eat with:
Endive & watercress salad
 (page 69) in my honey &
 mustard dressing
 (page 140)

This isn't just about a classic tomato sauce. It's about a classic tomato sauce with the coolest chicken dish. The amount of flavor going on is totally ridiculous—if you're a tomato fan, you've just got to make it.

Directions

1. Preheat oven to 425°F.
2. If the chicken breasts are very plump, lay a stretch of plastic wrap out on a board. Slap a piece of chicken on top. Cover with plastic wrap. Bash the chicken to flatten it a bit using a rolling pin or the palm of your hand. Don't make it too thin, as you need to stuff it.
3. Cut the chicken laterally across to create a pocket in the side.
4. Put your ham, cheese, and optional basil leaf in the pocket. Press the edges of the chicken well to seal. Season with salt, pepper, and garlic. Repeat.
5. Put the flour onto a large plate and the beaten eggs in a shallow dish or bowl. Spread the breadcrumbs on another plate.
6. Heat a bit of oil and butter in a large frying pan.
7. Dip each filet into the flour, then the egg, then the crumbs till covered. Fry for 2 to 3 minutes on each side to seal.
8. Bake on a greased baking sheet for 10 to 15 minutes. Test with a sharp knife to check that each filet is white all through and moist.
9. Heat the tomato sauce. Slap over or around the chicken.

Eggplant Roll-Ups in Tomato Sauce

A classic Italian dish. Soft strips of eggplant get stuffed with melting cheese 'n' herbs, then layered in a full-on tomato sauce. Get on your cell phone and get some mates over.

Directions

1. Sauce: Heat the olive oil gently in a pan. Cook the garlic and onion for 5 minutes or till soft, not colored. Add the tomatoes, sugar, salt, and pepper.

2. Reduce heat. Simmer gently for 15 to 20 minutes. If it gets too thick, add a splash of water. Taste. Add the lemon juice. Adjust seasoning.

3. Eggplant: Meanwhile, slice each eggplant into 5 to 6 thin lengths.

4. Slap the flour on a large plate. Pour the eggs into a large shallow dish.

5. Tip a few glugs of oil into a large frying pan. Heat gently.

6. Dip the eggplant slices into flour and then egg till coated. Increase heat. Fry slices for 1 to 2 minutes on each side or till golden. Rest on paper towels.

7. Preheat oven to 400°F.

8. Assembly: Spread a bit of tomato sauce in the base of a large, shallow ovenproof dish.

9. Sprinkle each eggplant slice with salt, pepper, and Parmesan. Add a basil leaf and a small slice of mozzarella or a teaspoon of grated halloumi. Roll each eggplant slice over the filling. Place the seam down on the tomato sauce. Repeat. Save half the mozzarella for topping.

10. Cover the rolls with the remaining sauce. Top with mozzarella, Parmesan, and a drizzle of oil. Bake for 20 minutes or more till hot and bubbling.

Serves 4

Ingredients

Tomato sauce

4 tablespoons good olive oil
1 to 2 cloves garlic, crushed
1 small onion, finely chopped
14-ounce can chopped tomatoes or plum tomatoes, drained
Pinch of sugar
Salt and pepper
Squeeze of lemon juice

Veg roll-ups

2 large, firm, shiny eggplants
3 tablespoons flour
2 eggs, beaten
Olive oil for frying
Salt and pepper
3 to 4 tablespoons freshly grated Parmesan
Bunch of fresh basil
12 ounces fresh sliced mozzarella, or
4 ounces grated halloumi plus 9 ounces fresh sliced mozzarella
Extra Parmesan and olive oil for topping

Eat with:

Warm crusty bread and green salad (page 140).

Why Not?

Fry 2 slices of eggplant till soft in a little garlicky olive oil. Season lightly. Lay between slices of focaccia or panini with sliced mozzarella, arugula, and smearings of tapenade or a drizzle of olive oil. Grill till cheese is soft and melty.

Tuna & Mash with Tomato

Serves 2
Ingredients
Mash
1 pound potatoes
1 clove garlic, peeled
¼ cup milk
2 tablespoons butter
Lemon juice
Any herb
Salt and pepper
Drizzle
1 teaspoon Dijon mustard
Pinch of sugar
1 tablespoon red wine or
   sherry vinegar
¼ cup olive oil
Pinch of salt
2 to 3 tomatoes, chopped
6 black olives, chopped
   (optional)
1 to 2 tablespoons chopped
   dill (optional)
Tuna
Olive oil
Garlic, peeled
Two ⅓-pound tuna steaks

Simply lovely. Simply healthy. Fresh tomato in a punchy dressing complements grilled tuna beautifully.

Directions
1. **Mash:** Bring a pan of lightly salted water to boil. Peel the potatoes and cut into large chunks. Add along with the garlic to the boiling water.
2. Boil for 20 minutes or till tender. Test by poking the spuds with a knife.
3. Drain. Slap back into the warm pan on low heat. Shake the pan to dry them for a minute without scorching.
4. Add the milk and butter to the pan to warm. Remove from heat. Mash the spuds and garlic with a masher or fork till ultra smooth. Add a good squeeze of lemon juice, any herb, and lots of salt and pepper. Cover and keep warm.
5. **Drizzle:** Whisk the mustard, sugar, vinegar, oil, and salt together. Add the tomatoes, along with olives and dill, if using.
6. **Tuna:** Rub a grill or frying pan very lightly with oil. Put it on to heat.
7. Mix the olive oil and garlic. Rub it into the tuna.
8. Slap the fish onto a sizzling hot pan or grill. Press down with a spatula so that it marks up well. Cook for 2 to 3 minutes per side, but don't overcook. Tuna is at its most tender when still pink in the middle.
9. **Assembly:** Slap a heap of lovely creamy mash on each plate. Top with the fish and a drizzle of tomato dressing. Perfect with green leaves and green beans.

Variations
DRESSED SALMON WITH TOMATO
At STEP 7, brush ssalmon filets with a mix of soy, sugar, and Chinese rice wine or rice vinegar. At STEP 9, top with tomato drizzle and bits of sushi ginger.
EXTRA FANCY
Top tuna or salmon with a mix of crème fraîche and chopped green onion and tomato.

Tomato & Mushroom on Polenta

I reckon this makes a perfect summer dish. Tomatoes are definitely at their best when they're just picked. Crisp grilled polenta is easy and makes an impressive addition. This is simple to make yet chic and delicious.

Directions

1. Polenta: Boil the water and salt in a large pan. Add the polenta or cornmeal in a steady stream. Stir with a long-handled spoon or whisk. Caution: it spits and bubbles. Reduce heat. Simmer for 5 minutes. Add butter, cheese, and herbs, if using.

2. Pour while hot into a lightly oiled pan approximately 11 x 7 x 1¼ inches, or over wax paper. Leave to cool.

3. Cut into fingers or squares when firm. Chill in fridge if not using immediately.

4. Topping: Set the tomato and mushrooms in a baking dish. Mix the garlic into the olive oil and brush over the vegetables. Leave to marinate for a while, or use immediately.

5. Preheat oven to 400°F.

6. Bake the tomato halves and mushrooms for 15 minutes.

7. Meanwhile, heat a grill or frying pan till hot. Brush the polenta squares with olive oil. Slap them on to sizzle. Don't turn till browned and crisp. Cook on all sides.

8. Assembly: Put a slice of polenta on each plate. Top with arugula, mushroom, and tomato. Drizzle with a little balsamic vinegar and oil.

Serves 2
Ingredients
Polenta
5 cups water
½ teaspoon salt
1½ cups polenta or cornmeal
4 tablespoons butter
2 handfuls of grated Parmesan (optional)
2 tablespoons chopped fresh sage or rosemary (optional)

Topping
1 large tomato, halved
2 portobello mushrooms
1 clove crushed garlic
Olive oil
Handful of arugula
Balsamic vinegar

Cheese

Henry's the biggest cheese fan I've ever met. A visit to his place means compulsory cheese-tasting sessions. But weirdly enough, he never cooks with it. Why not? In my book, it's a cracking ingredient. Cheese does stuff nothing else can. It melts down in a beautiful gooey style that spreads and pulls whatever it's cooked with together. It works as the main feature or in the background (like Henry's drumming). So grate it, slice it, melt it, or spread it. Crumble it. Chew it. Make it. Bake it. All that calcium and protein's really good for you. Stick it on bread and crackers. Slap it on pizzas. Chuck it on salads. Feature it in my Lancashire cheeseburgers or in a classic tart or two. Sharpen up a Greek phyllo pie with it. Whack it into French-style Yorkshire puddings, lovely Swiss cheese fondue, or on cheeky cheesy fish. Check out the cool Cheddar, chili, and onion muffins. Make your own cream cheese. Try a range of cheeses. Preferably local. Check out their weird names for a good laugh. Visit the deli and the farmer's market. You'll meet some great people who know about food and get some free tasting sessions. Enjoy yourself!

Makes 1 ball
Ingredients
1 teaspoon salt
2½ cups plain yogurt

Eat with:
Celery, carrots, or endive
  leaves
Bread and crackers
Cucumber sandwiches
Toast and raspberry jam
Honey on a sliced fruit plate

Fresh Cream Cheese

Sounds tricky? Don't you believe it. Making your own cream cheese is so easy. Customize with herbs or garlic, or eat as is. Drizzle with olive oil. Team with fruit for a quality breakfast.

Variation
SWEET CHEESE
CRÊPES
Slap sugar to taste into cream cheese. Spoon into a hot plain or chocolate crêpe (page 111). Drizzle with maple syrup and raspberries.

Directions
1. Set a large strainer or colander over a bowl. Line the strainer with a square of muslin (at least 18 inches in diameter).
2. Stir the salt into the yogurt (in a tub or measuring jug). Tip onto the muslin.
3. Either: leave in a cool place while the liquid (whey) drips through the strainer, leaving the cheese (curds) in the muslin. Or: Bring the ends of the muslin together. Tie over a tap so that the liquid drips into the sink.
4. Leave for 6 hours or overnight. Enjoy as is or customize it with seasoning.

Homestyle Poppy-Seed Crackers

Impressive. Cracking crackers (excuse the cheesy pun). Snack on these anytime you like. Perfect with toppings or dips for partying. Cheese and crackers is a classic pleaser.

Directions

1. Preheat oven to 300°F. Grease 2 large baking sheets.
2. Sift the flour, baking powder, and salt into a big bowl. Chuck the butter in.
3. Use your fingertips to rub the butter lightly into the flour till invisible. Stir in the poppy seeds.
4. Work in the half-and-half and water (you may not need it all) with a fork for a firm dough. Less water makes a crisper cracker.
5. Roll out (very thinly—less than half a centimeter) on a lightly floured board with a floured rolling pin. Prick all over with a fork to stop it from puffing when cooking. Cut into cracker shapes.
6. Cook on baking sheets for 25 to 30 minutes or till crisp and only just colored. Cool on a rack. Store in something airtight. Easy.

Makes 20
Ingredients
1¾ cups flour
½ teaspoon baking powder
½ teaspoon salt
2 tablespoons butter and extra for greasing
1 tablespoon black poppy seeds
1½ tablespoons half-and-half
5 to 6 tablespoons water

Variations
SALTY
Sprinkle with a bit of sea salt before baking.
ROSEMARY
Substitute chopped rosemary for poppy seeds.

White Cottage Loaf

Makes I large loaf
Ingredients
5 cups white bread flour
I teaspoon salt
I teaspoon sugar
I tablespoon butter
I packet (0.25 ounce) active
  dry yeast
1¾ cups warm water
Beaten egg and milk for
  brushing (optional)
Extra flour for dusting
  (optional)

Variations
NEAT PEOPLE'S
LOAF
At STEP 7, slap the
dough into a greased
2-pound loaf pan.

BRAID
At STEP 7, divide the
dough into three
strips. Join at one end
and braid together.

This classic old-style loaf shows off top cheeses (and cheers up average stuff). Think fantastic texture and awesome taste combo. Shape how you want it.
Pair with your favorite cheese.

Directions
1. Sift the flour, salt, and sugar into a big bowl.
2. Rub the butter into the flour using your fingertips till invisible.
3. Tip the yeast in. Add the water gradually, mixing with your hands or a metal spoon. Pull into a soft dough, adding a bit more water or flour if needed.
4. Using an electric mixer with a dough hook, knead for 5 minutes, or punch, slap, stretch, and knead by hand on a floured board for an 8-minute workout till pliable.
5. Rest the dough to rise in a large bowl somewhere warm till it's doubled in size. Cover with a tea towel.
6. Set the dough back on the board. Knead again for a minute.
7. Cut and mold two-thirds of the dough into a large bun shape. Set on a lightly floured baking sheet with the final third shaped into a smaller bun on top. Poke a wooden spoon handle down through the center to bond the two.

8. Cover loosely and leave to rise for 20 minutes. Preheat oven to 450°F.
9. **Crunchy crust:** Brush with the beaten egg and milk mix. **Soft crust:** Sprinkle a bit of extra flour over it.
10. Bake for 30 to 40 minutes. Stick parchment paper on top if it browns up too fast. Tap the bottom (it should sound hollow). Give it longer if needed. Cool on a rack. Eat with butter... and cheese.

Irish Soda Bread

A cool swap for regular bread if you're short on time and want a bit of a kick (the buttermilk does it). Made from scratch (no rising) in 40 minutes. Perfect match with hard and soft cheeses.

Directions
1. Preheat oven to 425°F.
2. Sift the flours, cream of tartar, baking soda, and salt into a large bowl.
3. Slap the butter in. Rub it into the flour lightly between your fingers till it's invisible.
4. Dig out a hole. Stir the buttermilk into the hole a bit at a time, incorporating the flour as you go for a soft dough. Add a splash more liquid if needed. Pull the dough together gently.
5. Set it on a lightly floured board. Handling gently (no kneading), shape it into a round loaf. Mark into 4 sections by cutting a cross into the top with a knife or press across with the handle of a wooden spoon.
6. Bake on a lightly greased baking sheet for 25 to 30 minutes or till the loaf looks done and sounds hollow when you tap the base.
7. Cool on a rack. Break into sections for serving. Best eaten the same day.

Makes 1 loaf
Ingredients
2 cups white flour
2 cups whole wheat flour
2 teaspoons cream of tartar
2 teaspoons baking soda
1 teaspoon salt
4 tablespoons soft butter
1¼ cups buttermilk (you may need a bit more)

Eat with:
Jam and butter

Variations
SODA WHITE
Use all white flour.
SODA BROWN
Use all whole wheat.

Spanakopita: Greek Cheese Phyllo Pie

Make it with mates. Eat it with mates. Laying out the phyllo is a two-person job. This crisp phyllo pie has the distinctive taste of salty feta with loads of spinach and garlic.

Directions

1. Preheat oven to 450°F.
2. **Filling:** Heat the oil in a big saucepan. Cook the onion and garlic gently. Stir with a wooden spoon for 5 minutes or till soft, not colored.
3. Pile the spinach in. It looks mountainous but wilts fast. Stir to coat. Soften for 2 minutes.
4. Tip into a big bowl with the feta, nutmeg, salt, and pepper. Mix thoroughly and adjust seasoning to taste.
5. **Pie base:** Melt the butter in a pan gently without coloring. Get a pastry brush.
6. Open the phyllo dough. Set it on a board or plate and cover with a tea towel or cloth to keep it usable.
7. Butter the base and sides of a 9-inch loose-bottomed tart pan. Lay the first sheet across it. Brush immediately with butter. Lay the next sheet across it to make the shape of a cross. Brush with butter. Repeat the pattern until 5 sheets are used.
8. **Filling:** Discard any liquid from the spinach/cheese mix. Spoon the filling over the pie base.
9. **Topping:** Lay a new sheet of phyllo across the pie. Brush with butter. Fold the edges down and in to seal the top and base together.

10. Lay another sheet to make the shape of a cross again. Butter. Fold down and in. Repeat with another 3 sheets till covered.
11. Remove the tart rim carefully. Put the pie on its base onto a baking sheet.
12. Brush the top with butter. Sprinkle with the poppy seeds and sea salt.
13. Bake for 15 minutes or till crisp and golden. Eat hot, warm, or cold.

Serves 4

Ingredients

1 to 2 tablespoons olive oil
1 medium-to-large onion, finely chopped
3 cloves garlic, peeled and crushed
1 pound baby or regular spinach leaves with any tough stalks removed
2⅓ cups crumbled feta cheese
Pinch of grated fresh nutmeg
Pinch of salt and pepper
2 tablespoons butter
8-ounce pack of phyllo pastry (10 sheets at least)
Poppy seeds and sea salt for topping

Eat with:
Tzatziki (page 140)
Baba ghanoush (page 90)
Greek salad
Toss chopped tomatoes, olives, and cucumber in an olive-oil-and-lemon dressing.

Serves 2
Ingredients
2 potatoes
1 tablespoon olive oil
Sea salt
1 tablespoon butter
2 white-fish filets, skin on
(cod or haddock, ⅓ pound
or as big as you like)
1 to 2 tablespoons pesto
(page 139)
3 to 4 tablespoons freshly
grated Parmesan
Homestyle ketchup
(page 139)
Malt vinegar

Eat with:
Mushy peas
Mush peas with a blender
or masher. Add some milk
or cream, a bit of chopped
fresh mint, and a squeeze of
lemon.

Cheesy Fish & Chips

Another fine multicultural feast. If you can't get to the
sea, make this—you'll be there. Tasty Italian pesto and
Parmesan lift the fish. Fat fries and peas bring it home.
Not a Parmesan fan? Try Cheddar.

Directions
1. Preheat oven to 425°F.
2. Fries: Boil the potatoes for 10 minutes. Drain. Cut into large oven
fries. Roll them in the olive oil and sea salt.
3. Lay on a baking sheet. Cook for 30 to 40 minutes.
4. Fish: Ten minutes before you eat, melt a bit of the oil and butter in a
frying pan till hot. Fry the fish, skin side down, for 3 to 4 minutes till it's
crispy.
5. Move the fish carefully onto a baking sheet using a spatula.
6. Spread a thin layer of pesto over the top of each filet. Sprinkle
generously with Parmesan.
7. Cook in the oven for 5 minutes or till white, cooked through, and
flaky. Pierce with a knife to check. (Larger portions can take way longer.)
Serve with fries, homestyle ketchup, and a bit of malt vinegar. Try it
with mushy peas for a real British meal!

Swiss Cheese Fondue

Creamy, cheesy, dead luxurious. Fondue's a posh cheese sauce to dunk chunks of bread in. It's speedy to prep and easy to do. Get a load of mates around for a fondue party.

Directions

1. Prepare all the ingredients and accompaniments before you get cooking.
2. Rub the cut garlic all around the inside of a saucepan or fondue pot.
3. Tip the wine in and heat till it just simmers. Don't rush it.
4. Add the cheese bit by bit, stirring constantly with a wooden spoon. It takes time to melt down to a smooth sauce between additions.
5. Put the water into a small bowl with the cornstarch. Mix together.
6. When the fondue mix eventually bubbles (don't let it burn), stir in the liquid cornstarch mixture, pepper, and nutmeg. Keep stirring as it thickens.
7. Very carefully carry the pot and set over a fondue burner on low heat.
8. Stick warmed bread onto fondue forks. Dunk. Eat 'em. Stir cheese occasionally.

Serves 4
Ingredients
1 large clove garlic, halved
1½ cups white wine
2 cups each shredded Gruyère and Emmentaler cheeses
1 tablespoon water
1 tablespoon cornstarch
Pepper
Freshly grated nutmeg
Best baguette or crusty bread in bite-size cubes
Other dunkers
Boiled new or fingerling potatoes

Eat with:
Tomato & onion salad (page 141)
Green salad (page 140)

Brilliant White Pizza

Serves 2
Ingredients
Pizza bases
2 to 4 frozen pizza bases, or make fresh:
3⅓ cups white bread flour
1 teaspoon salt
1 teaspoon sugar
2 packets (0.25 ounce each) active dry yeast
1¼ cups warm water
2 tablespoons olive oil
Topping
Olive oil
Cut clove of garlic
2 large balls mozzarella
Sea salt

Eat with:
Green salad (page 140)
Zucchini ribbon salad (page 141)
Mediterranean salad
Toss together 2 fresh chopped tomatoes, a few black olives, and a handful of arugula or spinach with a glug of olive oil and a drizzle of balsamic vinegar.

Variation
FOUR-CHEESE AND TOMATO
At STEP 7, spread garlicky tomato sauce, (page 55) over each base. Cover each quarter with a grated cheese of your choice, e.g., Gruyère, mozzarella, Parmesan, or Cheddar. At STEP 8, bake for 10 to 12 minutes or till crisp and bubbling.

Some people like their pizza with a lot of cheese. Doing it this way will really please the cheese lovers in your life. It's simple yet sophisticated—pure white pizza.

Directions
1. Fresh dough: Sift the flour and salt into a bowl. Add the sugar, yeast, water, and oil. Mix to a soft dough with your hand or a wooden spoon. Add more water or flour if needed.
2. Use an electric mixer with a dough hook for 8 minutes or slap the dough onto a floured board. Pull, stretch, and punch using the heel of your hand for 8 to 10 minutes to get it soft and elastic.
3. Move the dough to a bigger bowl. Cover with a paper bag or tea towel. Leave in a warm place for 1 hour or till doubled in size.
4. Lightly oil 2 to 4 large baking sheets. Slap the dough onto a board. Knead for 2 minutes. Cut into 2 or 4 pieces. Roll or punch and stretch each piece out thinly for bases.
5. Lay the bases on the baking sheets. Leave covered to rise for 15 to 20 minutes.
6. Preheat oven to 475°F.
7. Top: Brush fresh or frozen bases with a bit of oil. Rub with the cut garlic. Slice the mozzarella thinly. Lay over the bases with spaces for spreading.
8. Drizzle with a bit of oil and a sprinkle of sea salt. Bake for 15 minutes or till base is crisp and top is melted and just coloring.
9. Side: Meanwhile, make a salad. Serve with the pizza.

Cheese & Potato Pizza

A bit like Henry and music, these tastes go together. Think thin, crispy pizza base with a meltingly soft top. This comforting pizza's pretty spectacular.

Directions

1. Make fresh pizza dough (page 34) through STEP 3.
2. Boil the potato slices for 5 minutes. Don't let them break up. When just softening (test with a knife), drain well.
3. Gently fry the onion in oil till just soft, not colored.
4. Slap the pizza bases onto baking sheets. Spread the onion then crème fraîche or sour cream and herbs evenly over them.
5. Top with the potato slices. Layer the sliced cheeses over and in between the spuds with the optional sliced artichoke. Finish with more herbs, Parmesan, salt and pepper, and a little olive oil.
6. Bake for 10 to 15 minutes or till the base is crisp and the top bubbling.

Serves 2
Ingredients
2 frozen pizza bases or fresh (page 34)
2 large unpeeled potatoes (russet or Yukon Gold work) cut in ¼-inch slices
1 medium onion, thinly sliced
3 to 4 tablespoons olive oil and extra for drizzling
3 tablespoons crème fraîche or sour cream
Fresh chopped thyme or oregano
1 large ball mozzarella, thinly sliced
3 ounces (⅔ cup) thinly sliced Gruyère
Artichoke heart from a deli counter or jar, sliced (optional)
Freshly grated Parmesan
Salt and pepper

Eat with:
Coleslaw (page 140)
Watercress or arugula
Tomato salad (page 141)
Orange salad (page 140)
Roast pepper salad (page 140)

Variation
DIFFERENT TOPPERS
Try any of these as toppings: sun-dried tomatoes, smoked ham, pancetta, olives, rosemary.

Sfinciuni: Cheese-Pizza Pasty

Serves 1
Ingredients
1 small piece of pizza dough (page 34 through STEP 3)
1 to 2 tablespoons tomato sauce (page 55) or passata with a little crushed garlic
Bits of cooked ham, bacon, or salami
A few pitted olives
Any cheese, sliced or shredded
Fresh basil
Freshly grated Parmesan
Olive oil
Sea salt

Eat with:
Coleslaw (page 140)

Variation
CHEESE & HAM PASTY
Use buttery puff pastry in place of pizza dough. Roll out to a thin rectangle. Spread a little mustard on the bottom half. Cover with grated cheese, ham, and more grated cheese. Fold and brush with beaten egg and milk. Bake for 15 to 20 minutes. Good with a salad.

Pizza or pasty? Who cares? With brilliant tastes like these, there's no need to shell out for inferior store-bought pizza—or pasty. Perfect for snacks, meals, picnics. . . .

Directions
1. Roll the dough out thinly to a large rectangle on a floured board.
2. Smear the tomato sauce or passata thinly over the lower half.
3. Scatter your selection of meat, olives, cheese, basil, Parmesan, and a drizzle of olive oil over the sauce. Fold the top half over the lower half. Press the edges of the pasty down to seal (use a bit of water if needed).
4. Leave to rise in a warm place for 15 minutes.
5. Meanwhile, preheat oven to 425°F.
6. Brush the pasty with a bit of oil. Sprinkle with sea salt. Bake on a lightly oiled baking sheet for 10 to 15 minutes or till cooked through.

Gougère: French-Style Yorkshire

Two great cuisines collide. Yorkshire pudding meets French chic. Tasty, stringy cheese melts down into the best batter. Serve with salad or slice up for parties.

Directions

1. Whisk the eggs, salt, and milk furiously together with a hand whisk or electric mixer (whisk attachment). Leave 30 minutes if possible. Meanwhile, preheat oven to 425°F.

2. Tip 2 tablespoons of the oil into a casserole dish or pan (10 x 7 x 3 inches). Slap into oven in advance. You want it sizzling.

3. Sift and whisk the flour into the milk mixture till smooth, then add 2 tablespoons of oil. Whisk thoroughly.

4. Add the diced cheese to the batter.

5. Pour into the searing hot oil in the casserole dish. Cook for 35 minutes or till golden-topped and well risen. Chop into squares and eat as is (it's rich), or pair with chutney and salad.

Serves 4
Ingredients
2 eggs
Pinch of salt
1 cup milk
4 tablespoons sunflower oil
⅔ cup flour
8 ounces (1¾ cups) Gruyère cheese, diced into small cubes

Eat with:
Apple chutney for dipping (page 138)
Tomato & onion salad (page 141)
Green salad (page 140) with sharp dressing (heavy on the endive)

Classic Cheese & Onion Tart

Serves 4 to 6
Ingredients
Pastry
1 recipe pastry dough
   (page 138)
Filling
1 tablespoon light olive oil
4 tablespoons butter
3 large onions (about
   1½ pounds), thinly sliced
2 cloves garlic, crushed
3 eggs, beaten
1 cup sour cream
¾ cup shredded Gruyère
   or Cheddar
Salt and pepper

Variation
CHEESE, ONION, &
ASPARAGUS TART
At STEP 5, lightly fry
1 sliced medium onion
with a large bunch of
sliced green onions till
just soft. Steam or boil
10 asparagus spears till
just tender. At STEP 6,
mix the onion mix into
the sour cream and
cheese. At STEP 7, lay
half the filling in the
tart, add the cooked
asparagus on top like
wheel spokes, then add
the remaining filling.

This tart's a classic. A gorgeous mix of melted cheese and soft, sweet onions. Team with stuffed baked spuds and an awesome salad.

Directions
1. Make the pastry dough.
2. Grease a 9-inch loose-based tart pan.
3. Roll the pastry out lightly on a floured board. Make it big enough to fit the base plus sides of the pan.
4. Ease one edge of the pastry off the board. Roll the pin underneath to the center, then use it to lift the pastry up and over the pan. Let the pastry down onto the pan, then roll the pin away carefully. Mold the pastry gently into the pan. Fill any gaps with extra pastry. Press any tears together. Chill for 30 minutes.
5. Melt the oil and butter in a large pan over low heat. Cook the onions and garlic very slowly (20 to 30 minutes) till very soft but uncolored. Preheat oven to 400°F.
6. Set the onions aside to cool for a bit. Beat the eggs, sour cream, cheese, salt and pepper together. Mix in the onions.
7. Tip the mix into the tart. Bake for 30 minutes or till the pastry is cooked and the filling is risen and golden. Let it settle for 10 minutes before eating.

Variations
CHILI CHEESE
At STEP 1, chop in a
red chili pepper.
GREEK BURGER
Use feta cheese instead
of Lancashire and add
in a few chopped black

Serves 6
Ingredients
9 slices white crustless
  bread
1½ cups shredded
  Lancashire or Cheddar
  cheese
1 medium onion, finely
  chopped
2 tablespoons besan
  (chickpea flour)
1 to 2 tablespoons fresh
  chopped mint, basil, dill,
  parsley, or cilantro
1 large egg
1 teaspoon English or
  wasabi mustard
Grated rind of 1 lemon
Salt and pepper to taste
Sunflower oil

Dipping
Green salad leaves
Apple chutney (page 138)
Homestyle ketchup
  (page 139)
Homestyle mayos
  (page 139)

Stacking
Buns, pitas, or focaccia
Arugula
Thinly sliced tomato
Sliced red onion

Mashed avocado mayo
Mash half a ripe avocado
into 3 tablespoons mayo.
Mix in a crushed garlic clove
and a squeeze of lemon.

Lancashire Cheeseburgers

Who says burgers need meat? Here's the ultimate
tasty cheeseburger. Lancashire's sharpness of flavor
cooks up well. Get color and creativity into your

Directions

1. Blitz the bread to make crumbs. Tip them into a large bowl with
the cheese, onion, besan, and herbs.
2. Add the egg, mustard, lemon rind, salt, and pepper. Mix with a fork.
Chill the mix in the fridge till needed.
3. Sort the mayos and stacking ingredients before you start to cook.
4. Heat a little oil in a frying pan. Divide the mix into 6 flat burgers.
Fry gently for 4 minutes on each side or till cooked through and
golden.
5. Eat bread-free on a pile of any green leaves with apple chutney,
ketchup, and mayos for dipping, or eat in warm buns, pitas, or on

Blue Cheese Salad

Serves 2
Ingredients
Garlic croutons
1 clove garlic, crushed
1 tablespoon olive oil
1½ cups diced fresh bread
Salad
1 small red apple
A little lemon juice
2 crisp stalks celery
1 head endive or other
    lettuce
A few arugula or spinach
    leaves
A few walnuts (optional)
Dressing
4 ounces (½ cup) crumbled
    Roquefort cheese
¼ cup homestyle mayo
    (page 139)
½ cup crème fraîche or
    sour cream
1 teaspoon Dijon mustard
1 pinch sugar
1 clove garlic, crushed
1 tablespoon lemon juice

Eat with:
Warm crusty bread
    (page 28)

A French hero. Powerful flavors of garlic and Roquefort complement the crunchy textures in this creamy salad. P.S. I wouldn't recommend it before a date—it's a pungent one!

Directions
1. Preheat oven to 350°F.
2. **Garlic croutons:** Mix the garlic and oil in a bowl. Put the cubed bread in to coat. Slap them on a flat baking sheet. Crisp in the oven for 8 to 10 minutes.
3. **Salad:** Chop the apple into small pieces. Toss in a bowl with a bit of lemon juice (stops browning), then add thinly sliced celery, chopped endive, salad leaves, and optional nuts.
4. **Dressing:** Tip half the Roquefort into a blender, processor, or bowl. Blend or mash with other ingredients for smooth or rough texture. Taste. Adjust seasoning, adding a splash more water or lemon juice if you like it thinner.
5. Slap the salad onto plates. Cover with the dressing and remaining cheese. Top with the croutons. Store excess dressing in a jar and fridge it.

Variations
At STEP 3, add any of the following:
BLOODY MARY
3 diced sun-dried tomatoes and ½ teaspoon celery salt
GARLIC
3 gently fried tablespoons
CHORIZO
3 diced and fried slices
PANCETTA
3 crisp diced and fried slices
HAM & OLIVE
2 diced slices ham and pitted olives.
CREAMY
1 teaspoon cream cheese buried in each muffin

Cheddar, Chili, & Onion Muffins

Muffins don't need to be sweet—grate a strong Cheddar into this top savory mix. Great for late breakfasts and break-time snacks. Stick a few in your gym bag (don't crush 'em).

Directions

1. Preheat oven to 375°F. Meanwhile, tip the flour, baking powder, sugar, salt, cayenne, and mustard into a bowl.

2. Melt the butter gently in a small pan. Whisk the eggs and milk together in another bowl. Add the warm (not hot) melted butter.

3. Tip this liquid mix into the flour mix along with the cheese, onions, chili pepper, and herbs. Using a large metal spoon, fold the ingredients until they just come together. Don't beat the mix. You want to retain air. The odd lump is OK.

4. Split the mix between 12 large muffin liners on a baking sheet or in a muffin tin. Sprinkle Parmesan on top. Bake 20 to 30 minutes or till well risen and golden.

Serves 12
Ingredients
2¼ cups white flour, sifted
3 teaspoons baking powder
1 tablespoon suga
½ teaspoon salt
Good pinch of cayenne pepper
Pinch of dry mustard
4 tablespoons butter
3 eggs
1 cup milk
1⅓ cups shredded sharp Cheddar
4 green onions, finely sliced
1 small red chili pepper, de-seeded and finely chopped
Chopped fresh parsley, thyme, or cilantro
Grated Parmesan for topping

Eat with:
Soup
A bit of salad

Pasta

Ariyo loves pasta. Sometimes he'll have it three times a day when there's a game coming up, when he's training, or when he's just generally knackered. It gives him the energy he needs to excel at sports. Plus it's relaxing (the starch does it). Pasta's an easy, speedy thing to cook. Ideal for when he's had practice and then bused it back home at night. Don't think you need to be slapping fresh pasta together every time. Dried stuff from the deli or supermarket works fine. I've included the real deal for when you have the time and fancy a challenge. Vary your pasta (there're so many types). Always cook it in loads of lightly salted boiling water (it spreads). Sort a range of tasty sauces so that you're never bored. A while back, Ariyo's top sauce involved opening a jar—now he's into creamy

mushroom fettuccine and garlic bread, sausage ragu on penne (for breakfast), old family favorites like macaroni and cheese, crunchy garlic-breadcrumb linguine, angel-hair frittata, pasta al forno, and penne puttanesca. Team your pastas with some great little salads, crunchy breads, and freshly grated Parmesan.

Pasta with Sausage Ragu

Serves 4
Ingredients
1 tablespoon olive oil
1 onion, finely chopped
3 cloves garlic, peeled and crushed
1 small red chili pepper, de-seeded and chopped
1/2 teaspoon fennel seeds (or ground fennel)
6 quality pork or Italian sausages
3 1/4 cups roughly chopped button or crimini mushrooms
1/3 cup wine, water, or stock
14 1/2-ounce can diced tomatoes
1 teaspoon tomato purée
Pinch of sugar
Squeeze of lemon juice
2 tablespoons finely chopped parsley, rosemary, or basil
Pinch of salt
12 ounces fettuccine, penne, or farfalle (bow-tie) pasta
A bit of extra oil or butter (optional)
Parmesan for sprinkling

I can never quite finish this one, no matter how hungry I am. Maybe it's the carbs or that rich, meaty sauce. Perfect after a hard practice. Use quality sausages.

Directions

1. Heat the oil in a large pan. Chuck in the onion, garlic, chili pepper, and fennel seeds. Cook gently till soft and translucent.
2. Cut down the length of each sausage. Strip and discard the skin. Crumble or cut the meat into the onion mixture.
3. Increase heat. Stir the meat till it browns. Decrease heat. Slap in the mushrooms. Cook a further 5 to 10 minutes, stirring occasionally.
4. Increase heat. Add the wine, water, or stock. Boil for 2 to 3 minutes. Add the tomatoes, purée, sugar, lemon juice, and herbs.
5. Boil for 1 minute. Reduce heat. Simmer very gently for 15 to 20 minutes. Stir once or twice. Add a splash of liquid if it dries out.
6. Meanwhile, heat a large pan of lightly salted water to boiling. Add the pasta and cook as directed. Drain in a colander. Slap back in the pan with a bit of oil or butter if you like.
7. Stir the sauce in or serve on top of pasta. Eat with freshly grated Parmesan, bread, and a sharply dressed green salad.

Mushroom Pasta & Garlic Bread

If you're into mushrooms, this is your dish. Easy enough for every day, special enough for special occasions.

Directions

1. Garlic bread: Preheat oven to 400°F. Chuck the butter and crushed garlic in a bowl. Cream together. Mix in the chopped herbs and/or lemon juice, if using. Slash the loaf diagonally, leaving the pieces attached at the bottom. Spread the garlic butter into the cuts.

2. Wrap the bread in foil. Bake on a baking sheet for 25 minutes.

3. Pasta: Bring a large pan of lightly salted water to a boil. Add the pasta. Cook as directed.

4. Sauce: Meanwhile, heat the oil and butter gently in another pan.

5. Slap in the onion and garlic. Cook very gently for 5 minutes till soft but not colored. Add the mushrooms. Cook gently until they soften.

6. Increase heat as you pour in the wine, stock, or juice. Let the mixture bubble for 1 to 2 minutes so it reduces by half and looks sticky.

7. Stir in the cream or crème fraîche, reducing heat. Let it warm through and thicken. Add the parsley or tarragon.

8. Drain your pasta into a colander. Slap it back in the warm pan.

9. Chuck the mushroom cream over it and mix gently. Plate it. Sprinkle with the Parmesan. Eat with garlic bread.

Serves 2

Ingredients

Garlic bread

Lots of soft butter

2 to 3 garlic cloves, peeled and crushed

Chopped fresh herbs (optional)

Squeeze of lemon (optional)

1 loaf French bread

Pasta

8 ounces fettuccine

Sauce

1 tablespoon olive oil

2 tablespoons butter

1 small onion or 2 shallots, finely chopped

2 cloves garlic, crushed

10 ounces (4 cups) sliced white or button mushrooms

½ cup white wine, stock, or apple juice

⅓ cup heavy cream or crème fraîche

A bit of fresh parsley or tarragon, finely chopped

Freshly grated Parmesan

Eat with:

Green salad (page 140)
Tomato salad (page 141)

Why Not?

Make cheese-garlic mushrooms on toast. Make up half the sauce. Stick it on a piece of baked bread. Top with grated Gruyère. Stick it under the broiler in a small heatproof dish till bubbling.

Spaghetti with Oil, Garlic, & Chili

Serves 2
Ingredients
8 ounces spaghetti or
   linguine
4 tablespoons extra virgin
   olive oil
2 to 3 cloves garlic, peeled
   and finely chopped or
   crushed
1 to 2 red chili peppers,
   de-seeded, very finely
   chopped
Salt and pepper
Handful of flat-leaf parsley,
   finely chopped

Variation
CHILI POMODORO
At STEP 3, add 8
ounces chopped
cherry tomatoes, a
pinch of sugar, and
chopped parsley (or
basil, thyme, oregano,
or rosemary). Cook till
the tomatoes heat
through. Great with
croutons (page 10) or
garlic breadcrumbs
(page 47).

The simplicity of this dish is unbelievable, considering the amount of flavor it gives out. Chili peppers give the pasta a useful kick. Professional chefs make this for a workday lunch. Great to impress with little hassle.

Directions
1. Boil up a large covered pan of salted water.
2. Add the pasta. Boil and cook as directed till just soft with a bit of bite (al dente) or softer if you like. Test by trying a bit.
3. Meanwhile, heat the olive oil gently in a small pan. Add the garlic, chili pepper, and pepper. Sizzle on very low heat till soft. Don't let it color or burn, as it will taste bitter. Watch it.
4. Add the parsley and salt. Warm through for 15 seconds. Remove from the heat.
5. Drain the pasta in a colander.
6. Slap the pasta back into the warm pan. Mix the oil in. Serve.

Crunchy Garlic-Breadcrumb Linguine

I love this yummy, summery dish. The combo of lemon and crunchy garlic breadcrumbs really works. It's easy to figure out, so get cooking.

Directions

1. Put a large covered pan of salted water on to boil while you organize the other ingredients.

2. Add the pasta. Cover to bring to a boil. Cook as directed till the pasta is al dente or done to your liking.

3. Meanwhile, heat a little olive oil in a large pan. Fry the bacon or pancetta till crispy. Set it in a warm place on paper towels.

4. Garlic breadcrumbs: Blitz the bread into large crumbs in a food processor.

5. Take the pan you used to cook your bacon. Put it over low heat. Melt the butter and add the crushed garlic.

6. Tip the breadcrumbs in. Fry very gently, turning carefully with a spoon till the crumbs are crisp and golden. Keep them warm on a plate.

7. Drain the pasta into a colander. Slap the pasta back into the warm pan.

8. Add a drizzle of olive oil, bacon, tomatoes, parsley, arugula, lemon juice, pepper, half the Parmesan, and the breadcrumbs. Mix. Serve topped with the remaining crunchy crumbs and Parmesan.

Serves 2
Ingredients
6 ounces linguine
A little olive oil
4 slices bacon, chopped
6 slices white bread, crusts removed
4 tablespoons butter
2 cloves garlic, crushed
8 to 10 cherry tomatoes, halved
2 to 3 tablespoons chopped parsley
Handful of arugula
Juice of half a lemon
Salt and pepper
⅔ cup Parmesan, grated

Why Not?
Slap garlic butter or garlicky tomato sauce on a frozen homestyle pizza base and bake it.

Variation
VEGGIE LINGUINE
At STEP 3 instead of bacon, slice and fry 6 ounces (2 cups) mushrooms in olive oil and garlic.

Penne Puttanesca

Serves 4
Ingredients
3 tablespoons olive oil
3 fat cloves garlic, peeled and crushed
1 red chili pepper, de-seeded and finely chopped
1 pound ripe tomatoes, roughly chopped, or 14½-ounce can diced tomatoes
Pinch of sugar
6 ounces (1¼ cups) pitted black olives
1 tablespoon drained capers
Salt and pepper
6 anchovy filets
1 pound penne or spaghetti
2 tablespoons torn basil or finely chopped parsley
1 cup shredded mozzarella (optional)

Eat with:
Garlic bread (page 45)
Endive & watercress salad (page 69)
Zucchini ribbon salad (page 141)

This one's like the Mediterranean in a bowl. Tomatoes, capers, and olives melt down into a thick, hard-core sauce that wraps itself around your penne or spaghetti. If you sometimes find pasta bland, this is most definitely the one for you.

Directions

1. Sauce: Heat the oil in a large pan over gentle heat. Slap in the garlic and chili pepper. Cook without coloring for 5 minutes or till softening.
2. Add in the tomatoes, sugar, olives, capers, pepper, and anchovies.
3. Simmer over low heat for 20 minutes. You want it thickened. Stir occasionally to avoid sticking.
4. Pasta: Bring a large pan of lightly salted water to boil with the lid on. Uncover. Add the pasta. Cover and boil again. Cook as directed.
5. Drain into a colander.
6. Tip the pasta back into the pan with a bit of olive oil.
7. Stir the herbs and optional mozzarella into the sauce. Taste. Adjust the seasoning.
8. Stir the sauce into the pasta and plate it or put the pasta in bowls with the sauce on top.

Angel-Hair Frittata

Slice it up for hiking, picnics, slapping into a lunch bag, or really tasty anytime-eating. It's a thick omelette crossed with a pasta dish. Angel-hair pasta breaks down in the mix, creating a brilliant base for the salty tastes of olive and feta.

Directions

1. Bring a large pan of lightly salted water to boil. Add the pasta. Cook till just soft — 2 minutes. Drain. Set in a bit of cool water.

2. Heat half the oil gently in a 9-inch saucepan. Cook the onion, garlic, and chili pepper, stirring till softened, not colored. Tip the mix into a large bowl.

3. Drain the pasta thoroughly (pat dry if needed). Add to the onion mix with the feta, Parmesan, spinach or arugula, sour cream, optional olives, eggs, salt, pepper, and optional nutmeg to taste. Mix well.

4. Heat the remaining oil in the onion pan. Pour the frittata mix in. Cook over a gentle heat with a lid on for 10 minutes till just set through.

5. Heat broiler. Uncover the pan and slap it in the broiler to finish cooking (don't melt the handle!) for a few minutes till soft and golden.

6. Leave to settle. Eat hot, warm, or cold with salad.

Serves 4
Ingredients
$3\frac{1}{2}$ ounces angel-hair pasta
2 tablespoons olive oil
2 cups thinly sliced onion
3 cloves garlic, crushed
1 small red chili pepper, de-seeded and finely chopped
$1\frac{1}{3}$ cups crumbled feta
$\frac{1}{4}$ cup grated Parmesan
3 cups spinach or arugula
$\frac{2}{3}$ cup sour cream
A few black olives (optional)
6 eggs, beaten
Salt and pepper
Ground nutmeg (optional)

Eat with:
Green salad (page 140)
Tomato salad (page 141)
Tomato & onion salad (page 141)
Good crusty bread

Variation

At STEP 3, add bits of cooked ham or crisply cooked bacon or

DIY Pasta for Ravioli

Why not put aside an hour or two to slap on some music and make your own pasta? Use it to create these gorgeous, sweet-tasting ravioli in herb-and-butter sauce. Feeding the girlfriend? This is an impressive one....

Directions

1. **Pasta:** You can mix and pulse the pasta ingredients in a food processor, but it's best done by hand. Sift the flour and salt into a large bowl. Make a deep well in the center. Crack the eggs straight in. Whisk the eggs and then draw in the flour. Keep beating the mix until half the flour is incorporated.

2. Add the olive oil. Mix with your hands until you have a soft, stretchy dough and the flour's all in there.

3. Set it on a floured board. Knead it as you would for bread. Slap, stretch, pull, and roll it with the heel of your hand. After 5 to 10 minutes, you should get a smooth, elastic dough. Cover and leave for 20 minutes.

4. Roll the dough out as thinly as you can, using a rolling pin and a bit of stretching. Divide it into long rectangles almost as wide as the roller in your pasta machine. If you don't have one, keep rolling.

5. Set the machine up, clamping it to a table in order to leave both hands free to work. Or get a mate to hold it steady and help roll it. With the roller on its widest setting, insert the end of your first rectangle and roll it on through. Catch the rolled end as it emerges.

6. Roll pieces of dough until they are thin and still strong. Flour lightly if they stick. If they tear, you've over-rolled. Repeat with the remainder.

7. Divide the thin pasta up into squares approximately 3 x 3 inches with a sharp knife or pastry cutter. Leave them to dry out for 10 minutes.

8. Bring a large pan of salted water to boil for cooking the ravioli.

9. **Filling:** Mix the ricotta with the garlic, salt, pepper, Parmesan, and egg yolk.

10. Set a teaspoon of the cheese filling in the center of a pasta square. Put another square on top. Press gently around the mound of filling with your fingertips to seal. Repeat till all the pasta has been used up.

11. Put the ravioli in the boiling water. Cook for 5 minutes or till they rise to the surface. Remove with a slotted spoon. Drain in a colander.

12. **Sauce:** Working quickly, melt the butter gently in a pan. Add the lemon juice, sage, salt, and pepper. Pour over the plated ravioli. Scatter with Parmesan.

Serves 4
Ingredients
Pasta
2¼ cups flour
½ teaspoon salt
3 large eggs
1 tablespoon olive oil
Filling
1 cup ricotta
1 to 2 cloves garlic, crushed
Salt and pepper
⅔ cup grated Parmesan
1 egg yolk
Sauce
Butter
Juice of 1 lemon
Handful of fresh sage, chopped
Salt and pepper
Grated Parmesan

Variations
TOMATO PASTA
At STEP 1, add 1 tablespoon tomato purée.

TOMATO SAUCE
At STEP 12, use classic tomato sauce (page 55) instead of herb-and-butter sauce.

Why Not?
Cut the pasta into a few large sheets to use for lasagna (layer with ragu and top with cheese sauce), or put the pasta through the cutter on your machine for your own fettuccine.

Gingered-Up Sauce with Any Pasta

Serves 4
Ingredients
2 tablespoons olive oil
1 small onion, finely chopped
1 to 2 cloves garlic, crushed
Small piece of ginger, peeled
   and grated
14½-ounce can diced
   tomatoes
Pinch of sugar
Salt and pepper
Handful of fresh parsley,
   cilantro, or basil (optional)
Squeeze of lemon juice
1 pound pasta of choice
A little butter (optional)
Freshly grated Parmesan

Variations

GINGERED-UP
BRUSCHETTAS
Preheat oven to 400°F.
Drizzle olive oil over
slices of focaccia or
good white bread. Bake
on a baking sheet till
just crisp (5 to 10
minutes). Layer some
gingered-up sauce on
top. Top with a bit of
your favorite cheese.
Bake again till bubbling.

ROASTED TOMATO
& GINGER SAUCE
Preheat oven to 400°F.
Lay whole tomatoes in
a roasting pan with
sliced garlic and a little
grated ginger. Season
and drizzle with olive
oil. Roast 20 to 30
minutes or till they
blacken. Pull the skins
off with a fork. Blitz.
Pour over pasta with a
bit of extra olive oil,
fresh torn basil, and
grated Parmesan.

A classic tomato sauce meets ginger. Need I say more?
I don't think so. OK—slap it on your best pasta. Grate
Parmesan at the table for a top taste and a cool ritual.

Directions

1. Heat the olive oil in a pan. Add the onion, garlic, and ginger. Cook
gently for 5 minutes or till soft and translucent.
2. Tip the tomatoes in with the sugar, salt, and pepper. Stir and bring to
a boil. Reduce heat immediately. Simmer for 10 to 15 minutes.
3. Add the herbs, if using, and the lemon juice. Taste and adjust
seasoning.
4. Meanwhile, bring a large covered pan of lightly salted water to a boil.
Add your pasta of choice when the water is boiling. Cover as the water
returns to a fierce boil. Remove the lid and cook as directed.
5. Drain the pasta well and slap it back in the pan with a bit of olive oil
or butter. Mix in the sauce. Plate it or serve it in bowls with Parmesan.

Variations

BACON
At STEP 6, add a layer of cooked bacon on top of half the mixture. Top with the rest.

SPINACH
At STEP 6, put a layer of cooked spinach on the base of the dish.

MUSHROOM
At STEP 5, stir in some cooked mushrooms.

CAULIFLOWER
Cook cauli florets in lightly salted water till tender (8 to 10 minutes) and substitute for pasta.

BREADCRUMBS
At STEP 6, sprinkle a mix of extra cheese and 1 to 2 tablespoons fresh white breadcrumbs over the top. Bake till bubbling.

Good Old Macaroni & Cheese

You can't beat it. A favorite in our house and with everyone I know, so it doesn't need much introduction. Just make sure your sauce is properly cheesy and fully seasoned. Have a go at the green-bean spaghetti.

Directions

1. Put a large pan of salted water on to boil.
2. Slip the macaroni in. Cook as directed till just tender. Drain in a colander.
3. Preheat oven to 400°F.
4. **Cheese sauce:** Melt the butter in a small pan over gentle heat. Add the flour. Stir furiously with a wooden spoon for 2 minutes. Remove from heat. Pour the milk in gradually, beating well with a balloon whisk or spoon to make a smooth, thin sauce.
5. Return to heat. Bring it slowly to a boil while still beating. The sauce will thicken. Add a bit more milk if you think it needs it. Simmer for 2 minutes. Slap in the cheese, mustard, lemon juice, salt, and pepper. Stir and heat for another minute. Taste the sauce and adjust the seasoning.
6. Add the macaroni. Pour the mix into an ovenproof dish. Top with extra cheese. Bake for 20 minutes till golden.

Serves 4
Ingredients
6 ounces (1⅔ cups) macaroni
Cheese sauce
½ tablespoon butter
2½ tablespoons flour
1¾ cups milk
1½ cups shredded sharp Cheddar, plus a bit more for topping
½ teaspoon mustard
1 tablespoon lemon juice
Salt and pepper

Eat with:
Green-bean spaghetti
Thinly slice beans lengthwise. Boil for 3 to 4 minutes. Drain. Delicious— cutting them this way magnifies the flavor!

Pasta al Forno

Sounds fancy, but it's not. *"Al forno"* means baked. This is just like lasagna, but with stuffed pasta shells instead of sheets. The cheesy, tomatoey sauce is a winner. A great excuse for getting a load of mates around the table.

Directions

1. **Beef ragu filling:** Heat the butter and oil gently. Add the onion, celery, garlic, and a pinch of salt. Cook very gently over low heat in a covered pan to sweat the veg for 5 to 10 minutes.

2. Stir in the bacon. Cook for a minute, then increase heat.

3. Chuck in the beef, stirring till it browns all over.

4. Pour in the wine, if using, and let it bubble. Add the stock or water, tomato purée, lemon juice, and pepper. Boil the mix for a minute, then reduce heat to low. Let it simmer gently for at least 40 minutes, stirring occasionally. Don't let it dry out. Add a bit more liquid if it needs it. Add more purée if it's too runny. You want a thick sauce.

5. **Tomato sauce:** Meanwhile, heat the oil for the sauce in another pan. Add the onion or shallot, garlic, and a pinch of salt. Cook till soft, not brown.

6. Tip in the tomatoes, sugar, tomato purée, herbs, pepper, and lemon juice. Boil. Reduce heat. Leave to simmer, stirring occasionally. Add a little water if it gets too thick.

7. **Pasta:** Cook the pasta shells as directed till just tender. Drain them well.

8. Preheat oven to 400°F. Spread a thin layer of the tomato sauce over the base of an ovenproof dish.

9. Use a teaspoon to fill each pasta shell or tube with the meat mix. Set the filled pasta on top of the sauce. Sprinkle a little Parmesan over the top, followed by a layer of tomato sauce to cover.

10. Top the lot with a layer of mozzarella and Parmesan to cover. Cover very loosely with foil. Bake for 30 to 40 minutes.

Serves 4 to 6
Ingredients
Beef ragu filling
2 tablespoons butter
1 tablespoon oil
1 onion, finely chopped
1 stick celery, finely chopped
2 cloves garlic, crushed
Pinch of salt
2 slices bacon, chopped
¾ pound ground beef
¼ cup wine or stock
½ cup stock or water
2 teaspoons tomato purée
Squeeze of lemon juice
Pepper

Classic tomato sauce
1 to 2 tablespoons olive oil
1 small onion or 2 small
  shallots, finely chopped
2 cloves garlic, crushed
Pinch of salt
14½-ounce can diced
  tomatoes
Good pinch of sugar
1 tablespoon tomato purée
Handful of fresh basil, or
  parsley
Pepper
Squeeze of lemon juice

Pasta
16 conchiglioni (large pasta
  shells) or cannelloni tubes

Topping
3 to 4 tablespoons freshly
  grated Parmesan
10 ounces mozzarella, thinly
  sliced

Variations
Fill shells with:
TUNA & RICOTTA
Mix a drained can of tuna with a tub of ricotta cheese, 1 crushed garlic clove, a squeeze of lemon, and pepper.
MOZZARELLA & RICOTTA
Mix 1 ball of mozzarella, finely chopped, with 1 tub of ricotta, salt, pepper, and a bit of cooked, diced spinach.

Veg

Warning: this section's not just for vegetarians. Joe loves his meat as much as I do, but when it comes to top tastes, he's nuts for the green stuff. There's so much out there, it's a real vegetable field day. Vegetable cooking's a true test for a chef. You need to get creative with combinations of flavors and textures, using herbs and spices with skill and subtlety. These recipes are just the tip of the iceberg (lettuce). You've got curries, burgers, chili tortillas, risotto, moussaka, cool soups, baked endive, red cabbage, fritters, Sicilian caponata, and stand-alone vegetables that are truly magnificent. Joe grows his own 'cause the fresher the better. We're talking health gods (that's the veg, not Joe—

though he does play a mean game of soccer). Think fiber, energy, minerals, and vitamins to keep you going. No garden? No sweat. Get to farmers' markets or farm stands (Joe works at one) or old-style greengrocers. Always sniff and prod veg to check its credentials. Google it to check out when it's in season. Buying in supermarkets? Check that it's grown locally, not flown here on vacation.

Leek & Onion Soup

Serves 4
Ingredients
Soup
1 tablespoon butter
Glug of olive oil
¾ pound (4 cups) thinly
    sliced leeks
2 large onions, thinly sliced
2 to 3 cloves garlic, crushed
2 teaspoons sugar
Salt and pepper
1½ cups white wine,
    apple juice, or cider
3⅔ cups veg or chicken
    stock (page 138)
Topping
Baguette or ciabatta, sliced
Hot mayo (page 139)
A bit of crushed garlic
2 to 3 handfuls of grated
    Gruyère or Cheddar

A variation on classic French onion soup. Leeks make it sweeter. Team with crunchy cheese-and-harissa croutons. A real winter winner.

Directions

1. Melt the butter and oil in a large heavy-bottomed pan or casserole dish.

2. Add the leeks, onions, garlic, and sugar. Stir to coat in oil.

3. Sweat over low heat with the lid on till well softened, not colored (10 to 15 minutes). Add salt and pepper.

4. Increase heat. Stir the veg till they brown (don't let them burn).

5. Add the wine, juice, or cider. Let it bubble. Keep stirring.

6. Add the stock (plus extra if needed). Bring the soup to a boil for a minute, then simmer, covered, on low heat for at least 20 minutes but preferably longer for a deeper flavor. Taste and adjust the seasoning.

7. Croutons: Toast slices of bread, or smear with a bit of olive oil and bake in a hot oven till crisp (5 to 10 minutes).

8. Mayo: Stir a bit of crushed garlic into the hot harissa mayo.

9. Ladle the soup into bowls. Spread the croutons with the mayo. Top with the cheese and drop onto soup. Nice one.

Butternut Squash & Ginger Soup

This cheery soup offers instant comfort. Butternut squash is so good for you, and the Thai-style ginger, coconut, and lime combo gives it a great kick.

Directions

1. Preheat oven to 400°F. Slap the squash on a baking sheet. Drizzle with oil. Roast for 30 minutes or till soft.

2. Meanwhile, melt the butter gently in a large pan. Fry the onion and garlic for 5 minutes or till soft, not colored. Add the ginger. Remove from heat.

3. Add the cooked squash, lime juice, stock, coconut cream, cilantro, salt, and pepper to the mix.

4. Bring to a boil as you stir. Reduce heat. Cover. Simmer gently for 15 minutes. Top up with a bit more liquid if it looks too thick.

5. Blitz with a blender or processor. A hand blender works, too. Taste. Add more seasoning and/or lime, optional shakes of Tabasco, and/or balsamic vinegar and cilantro.

Serves 4

Ingredients

1½ pounds butternut squash, peeled and cut into chunks
Olive oil
2 tablespoons butter
1 medium onion, finely chopped
2 fat cloves garlic, crushed
4- to 5-inch piece of fresh ginger, peeled and grated
Juice of 2 plump limes
3⅔ cups veg stock (page 138)
3 tablespoons coconut cream dissolved in 1¼ cups boiling water
2 teaspoons chopped cilantro, plus extra for topping
Salt and pepper
Tabasco sauce (optional)
Balsamic vinegar (optional)

Eat with:
Grated Parmesan
Crumbled cooked pancetta or bacon
Warm soda bread or classic bread and butter

Variations

CHILI IT
Crumble 1 or 2 dried chili peppers over the squash before roasting.
SPICE IT
Sprinkle in 2 teaspoons cumin.

Endive au Gratin

Serves 4
Ingredients
1 lemon
4 endive heads
1 clove garlic, cut
Soft butter
Salt and pepper
4 thin slices ham (optional)
1 tablespoon Dijon mustard
½ cup heavy cream or
  crème fraîche
Grated Gruyère or
  Parmesan
Fresh breadcrumbs
  (optional)

Eat with:
Warm bread to mop juices
Tomato & onion salad
  (page 141)
Green salad (page 140)

Variation

BRAISED ENDIVE
At STEP 4, melt
1 tablespoon butter in
the dish. Remove. Lay
the endive in it. Season
with salt and pepper,
the juice of ½ lemon,
and ½ tablespoon
sugar. Lay a bit of
buttered parchment
paper (buttered side
down) on top. Cover
dish. Bake at 375°F for
30 minutes or till
tender. Eat as above or
as a side dish.

Why Not?

Chuck uncooked
endive leaves in to
roast for the last 30
minutes with a whole
chicken. The bottom
caramelizes, flavoring
spuds and gravy.

Endive's slightly bitter, so it really does the business in this cheesy, creamy sauce. Makes a great veggie dish without the ham. Complements a lovely roast chicken.

Directions

1. Boil up a pan of water large enough to fit the endive. Add a bit of salt and a squeeze of lemon. Trim the endive heads, if necessary.
2. Boil the endive for 5 minutes. Drain into a colander. Cool. Squeeze excess water out with a tea towel.
3. Preheat oven to 375°F.
4. Rub the cut garlic over the surface of a shallow baking dish. Butter well all over. Squeeze lemon juice in there.
5. Season the endive with pepper and lemon. Wrap it in the ham, if using.
6. Lay it in a dish. Cover with a mix of the mustard, cream or crème fraîche, salt, and more pepper, if desired. Sprinkle with the cheese and optional breadcrumbs.
7. Bake for 20 to 30 minutes till tender (test with a knife), bubbling, and golden. Fat endive heads may take longer.

Sweet Corn Fritters

These fritters have a bit of bite. Make them work as a snack with dips when you've got mates around or pile 'em high to go with fried chicken or vegetable chili.

Directions

1. Thaw frozen corn under warm water. Sift the flour, salt, and paprika into a bowl.

2. Make a dip in the center of the mix. Crack the egg in with a little of the milk. Beat together with a wooden spoon or balloon whisk.

3. Gradually add the rest of the milk, incorporating as you go for a thick, smooth batter. Rest it for 30 minutes—unless desperate!

4. Gently mix the corn, chopped peppers, and cilantro into the batter.

5. Heat the oil in a pan. Drop tablespoons of the fritter mix into the pan. Fry 1 to 2 minutes on each side till the top bubbles and the base is golden. Keep cooked fritters warm while the others are frying.

Serves 4
Ingredients
½ cup flour
Pinch of salt
Pinch of paprika
1 egg
⅓ cup milk
1 cup corn, frozen or cut off the cob
1 small red chili pepper, de-seeded and finely chopped
1 red pepper, de-seeded and finely chopped
A bit of chopped fresh cilantro
2 tablespoons sunflower or olive oil

Eat with:
Guacamole (page 139)
Sour cream
Tomato salsa (page 140)
Veggie chili (page 65)

Spicy Mushroom & Chickpea Burgers

Serves 6
Ingredients

3 tablespoons olive oil
$\frac{2}{3}$ cup finely chopped onion
2 cloves garlic, peeled and crushed
1 small dried chili pepper, crumbled
1 teaspoon ground cumin
1 teaspoon ground coriander
$\frac{1}{4}$ teaspoon turmeric
1 teaspoon lemongrass paste or $\frac{1}{2}$ piece fresh lemongrass, finely chopped
$2\frac{3}{4}$ cups finely chopped mushrooms
Juice of 1 lime
Salt and pepper
$15\frac{1}{2}$-ounce can chickpeas
$1\frac{2}{3}$ cups fresh breadcrumbs
A few shakes of Tabasco sauce
2 tablespoons finely chopped fresh cilantro
Flour for coating
Olive oil for frying

Stack

Griddled, toasted, or warmed bun or ciabatta
Guacamole (page 139)
Thinly sliced tomato
Mayo mixed with sweet chili sauce
Arugula
Chopped green onion

Share a plate of these superior burgers with a group of hard-core meat-eating mates and see if they moan (they won't). They taste a bit like falafel but much better.

Directions

1. Slap the olive oil in a large pan. Heat gently. Add the onion and garlic. Cook, stirring for 5 minutes, till softening—not colored.

2. Chuck in the chili peppers, cumin, coriander, turmeric, and lemongrass. Cook for 3 minutes. Add the mushrooms and lime juice. Cook for 5 minutes to soften. Season with salt and pepper. Tip into a large bowl to cool a bit.

3. Semi-blitz the chickpeas in a processor or crush with a fork till broken, not pasted. Add to the bowl with the breadcrumbs, Tabasco, cilantro, salt, and pepper. Mix well with a fork.

4. Scatter coating flour on a large plate. Flour hands. Take handfuls of the mix and gently shape into 6 burgers. Wash and re-flour hands if they get sticky.

5. Chill the burgers on a plate in the fridge for a few minutes.

6. Fry for 3 to 4 minutes on each side in a little olive oil. Check that they're cooked through. Set on salad leaves or stack 'em.

Ingredients
2 tablespoons sunflower oil
1 large onion, finely chopped
2 fat cloves garlic, peeled
   and crushed
2-inch piece fresh ginger,
   peeled and grated
1 chili pepper, de-seeded
   and finely chopped
6 cardamom pods, cracked
3 Kaffir lime or curry
   leaves, crumbled
1 pound (6½ cups) halved
   or sliced button
   mushrooms
1 tablespoon ground
   coriander
1 teaspoon chili powder
2 teaspoons cumin
2 good pinches turmeric
1 teaspoon sugar
1 cup chopped canned or
   fresh tomatoes
3 tablespoons cream,
   yogurt, or crème fraîche
2 tablespoons chopped
   fresh cilantro
Salt and pepper

Eat with
Basmati rice (page 84)
Naan bread
Poppadoms
Mango chutney

Mushroom Curry

Mushrooms can be a bit tame, but not when they're done this way. There's a lot of spice in here, so taste as you go to check that you've got a good balance of flavors. An awesome curry... add it to your repertoire.

Directions

1. Heat the oil in a large pan. Gently cook the chopped onion for 5 minutes or till softened but not colored.
2. Slap in the garlic, ginger, chili pepper, cardamom, and leaves. Stir around for a few minutes. Add the mushrooms and cook gently for 5 minutes.
3. Add the coriander, chili powder, cumin, turmeric, sugar, and tomatoes.
4. Cover. Simmer gently for 10 minutes.
5. Stir in the cream, yogurt, or crème fraîche, and the cilantro. Taste and season with salt and pepper.

Why Not?

Make some **raita.** Finely chop a 4-inch piece of cucumber. Mix with 1 chopped green onion, 2 crushed garlic cloves, 6 tablespoons yogurt, salt, and pepper.

Variation

CURRY WITH PEAS
Slap in some cooked peas at STEP 5.

Serves 4
Ingredients
1 big onion, finely chopped
3 cloves garlic, peeled and crushed
1 inch fresh ginger, peeled, roughly grated
1 to 2 red chili peppers, de-seeded and finely chopped
3 tablespoons peanut or sunflower oil
1 teaspoon ground cumin
1 teaspoon turmeric
2 teaspoons ground coriander
1 teaspoon garam masala
2 ripe tomatoes, chopped
½ cup tomato purée
1 cup water
1 large sweet potato, peeled and cubed
1 cauliflower, cut into florets
14-ounce can chickpeas
Salt
Juice of 1 lemon
Fresh cilantro

Eat with:
Basmati rice (page 84)
Grilled naan bread
Mango chutney
Raita (page 63)

Why Not?
Make spinach curry.
Slap 2 bags of baby spinach in a pan with 2 tablespoons water. Wilt for 2 minutes. Drain well. Squeeze out the moisture. Stir-fry 1 teaspoon mustard seeds in oil for 2 minutes (lid on pan). Add crushed garlic, sliced onion, and a pinch of curry powder. Cook gently till soft. Add the spinach and a bit of salt. Heat through.

Cool Cauli Curry

One to master before you leave home. It brings together a range of vegetables and chickpeas—great for protein. Strong on taste. Make a load on the weekend for weekday eating.

Directions
1. Mix the onion, garlic, ginger, and chili peppers together. Or blitz the lot with a bit of water in a food processor.
2. Heat the oil in a large heavy-bottomed pan. Add the onion mix and stir over medium heat with a wooden spoon for 2 minutes.
3. Add the cumin, turmeric, coriander, and garam masala. Stir and cook for another few minutes.
4. Reduce heat. Add the fresh tomatoes. Cook, stirring till they get pulpy.
5. Pour in the tomato purée and water. Mix well. Add the sweet potato, cauliflower, and chickpeas.
6. Cover and cook over gentle heat for 20 minutes or till the cauliflower is just tender. Add a bit more water if you think it needs it.
7. Remove the lid. Simmer gently for at least 10 minutes so the sauce reduces. Don't let it dry out. You may want to simmer it even longer.
8. Taste. Season with salt, lemon juice, and cilantro. Keep tasting. . . .

Chili Pepper & Bean Tortillas

I always use red or orange peppers, as a riper pepper gives a sweeter taste. Enjoy this macho chili wrap grilled, baked, or barbecued. Cool for lunch and supper. Great for parties.

Directions

1. Filling: Slap the oil into a large pan. Fry the onions and garlic very gently till softening but not colored. Stir in the peppers. Cook for 5 to 8 minutes till softening.

2. Add the chili peppers, cumin, beans, cayenne (or chili powder), paprika, sugar, tomatoes, purée, coriander, and water. Bring to a boil, stirring.

3. Reduce heat and cover the pan. Simmer for 20 minutes. Check that it's not sticking, and stir occasionally.

4. When the sauce is thick, taste and season with salt and pepper. Chill till needed.

5. Wraps: Lay the tortillas flat. Spoon a layer of the chili down the center of each. Sprinkle with the cheese. Roll each wrap around the filling. Roll foil around the wrap. Slap on a very hot pan or grill for 4 minutes or till cooked through or bake on a sheet at 425°F for 10 minutes. Eat from the foil wrapper.

Makes 12
Ingredients
Bean chili filling

2 tablespoons olive or sunflower oil
1 onion, finely chopped
2 cloves garlic, crushed
1 red pepper and 1 yellow pepper, de-seeded, cored, and chopped
2 small red chili peppers, de-seeded and finely chopped
1 teaspoon ground cumin
14½-ounce can (2 cups) red kidney beans, drained and rinsed
½ teaspoon cayenne or chili powder
1 teaspoon paprika
1 teaspoon sugar
14½-ounce can (2 cups) diced tomatoes
2 tablespoons tomato purée
2 tablespoons ground coriander
½ cup water
Salt and pepper

Wraps
12 small soft tortillas
Grated Cheddar

Eat with:
Guacamole (page 139)
Sour cream
Salsa (page 140)

Variation
VEGGIE CHILI ON RICE
At STEP 2, add a splash more water for a looser mix. At STEP 5, serve chili on bowls of rice with salsa, grated Cheddar, sour cream, guacamole, and lime for squeezing. Scoop up with soft warmed tortillas and tortilla chips.

Serves 4
Ingredients
6 tablespoons olive oil
2 eggplants cut in ¾-inch slices
Salt and pepper
3 stalks celery, thinly sliced
1 large onion, thinly sliced
14½-ounce can diced tomatoes or 1 pound (2½ cups) fresh tomatoes, skinned and chopped
⅓ cup raisins
⅓ cup pitted green or black olives
1 teaspoon capers
1 to 2 tablespoons sugar
4 tablespoons red wine vinegar
2 tablespoons finely chopped parsley
2 to 3 hard-boiled eggs, chopped (optional)

Eat with:
Warm crusty bread
Salads (pages 140 to 141)
Cheeses
Cold deli meats

Why Not?
Warm any leftovers. Stir in crème fraîche. Whack into any pasta you fancy.

Cracking Caponata

This is a classic Sicilian dish that brings out the best in eggplant. It's sort of sweet and sour but subtler than that. Serve it as a main course or salad. Scatter with chopped hard-boiled egg if you like.

Directions

1. Heat half the oil in a large pan. Fry the eggplant till soft. Season with a bit of salt and pepper. Cool on paper towels.

2. Reduce heat and slap the celery into the pan. Cook gently till just soft. Remove to cool on the paper towels.

3. Tip the remaining oil into the pan to heat. Add the onion. Cook gently for 5 minutes or till softened but not colored.

4. Add the tomatoes, raisins, olives, and capers. Season with pepper. Simmer gently with the lid on for 15 minutes.

5. Add the sugar and vinegar. Simmer for another 15 minutes.

6. Stir the eggplant and celery into the mix. Remove from heat.

7. Leave the caponata to rest for 30 minutes. Taste and adjust seasoning. Add the parsley and chopped eggs, if using. Eat at room temperature.

Red Cabbage with Apple & Spices

Red and purple veg have more health boosters in them than most. But forget that. This has a brilliant color, plus a mass of spicy, apple-y, sweet, and sour flavors. Try with potato cakes, pork, or sausages, to name just a few ideas. . . .

Directions

1. Preheat oven to 350°F.
2. Strip off and discard the covering leaves of the cabbage. Chop the rest in sections. Cut away the hard core. Discard. Shred the cabbage thinly.
3. Get a large casserole dish. Slap a covering layer of cabbage in the bottom. Season with salt and pepper. Layer in a third of the apple, then a third of the onion. Add the garlic, I tablespoon brown sugar, and a sprinkling of allspice.
4. Repeat layering till all the veg are used. Finish with a layer of cabbage.
5. Season again. Dot the butter over the top. Spoon the vinegar in there.
6. Cover and cook for I hour. Check and stir every 20 minutes. Test to see that it's the texture you like. Give it extra time if you think it needs it.

Serves 4
Ingredients
1 red cabbage
Salt and pepper
2 big cooking apples, peeled, cored, and chopped
2 big onions, chopped small
3 fat cloves of garlic, crushed
3 tablespoons brown sugar
2 teaspoons allspice
2 tablespoons butter
3 tablespoons wine vinegar (try raspberry vinegar)

Eat with:
Mash (page 22)
Sausages (veggie or otherwise)
Cooked bacon
Glazed ham (page 78)
Roast pork (page 83)
Cheesy potato cakes (page 94)

Why Not?
Make red cabbage salad. Shred a load of red cabbage. Slap in a bowl with I diced orange, I diced apple, I sliced avocado, and a few crushed walnuts. Make a dressing of mustard, honey, white wine vinegar, sunflower oil, and a bit of walnut oil. Toss it together. Tasty.

Vegetable Moussaka

A Greek feast. Layers of soft eggplant and potato in a cinnamon-tinged sauce and creamy topping. Perfect with tapas for big family dinners.

Serves 4
Ingredients
2 large potatoes, peeled
Olive oil
1 large onion, peeled and finely chopped
3 cloves garlic, crushed
Two 14½-ounce cans diced tomatoes
A splash of red wine
1 teaspoon dried or fresh chopped oregano
Pinch of cinnamon
Pinch of sugar
2 tablespoons tomato purée
15½-ounce can red kidney beans, drained and rinsed
2 eggplants, sliced
2 tablespoons chopped fresh parsley
Salt and pepper
Topping
1½ tablespoons butter
2½ tablespoons flour
1¾ cups milk
1 cup shredded Cheddar, plus extra for topping
½ teaspoon mustard
1 tablespoon lemon juice
Salt and pepper

Eat with:
Tzatziki (page 140)
Warm pitas
Green salad (page 140)
Tomato & onion salad (page 141)
Hummus (page 140)

Directions

1. Boil the spuds till just tender. Drain. Slice. Set aside.

2. Heat a bit of oil in a large pan. Cook the onion and garlic gently for 5 minutes or till softened, not colored.

3. Add the tomatoes, wine, oregano, cinnamon, sugar, and purée. Boil. Reduce heat. Cover. Simmer gently for 10 minutes. Add the beans. Simmer another 20 minutes. Taste and season with salt and pepper.

4. Meanwhile, heat 4 tablespoons of oil in a large frying pan. Fry batches of eggplant in a single layer till just soft and golden on each side. Remove to wait on paper towels. Preheat oven to 375°F.

5. Topping: Melt the butter in a small pan over gentle heat. Add the flour. Stir furiously with a wooden spoon for 2 minutes. Remove from heat. Pour the milk in gradually, beating well with a balloon whisk or spoon to make a smooth, thin sauce. Return to heat.

6. Bring the mixture slowly to a boil, still beating. The sauce will thicken. Add a bit more milk if you think it needs it. Simmer for 2 minutes. Slap in the cheese, mustard, lemon juice, salt, and pepper. Stir and heat for another minute.

7. Use 4 small, shallow heatproof dishes or 1 shallow dish approximately 9 x 9 x 2½ inches deep. Layer the tomato-bean mix, eggplant, grated cheese, potato, and so on. Finish with eggplant. Cover with the topping. Sprinkle with extra cheese.

8. Bake for 1 hour or till hot and bubbling. Rest for 10 minutes before eating.

Zucchini, Lemon, & Thyme Risotto

Hmm. Risotto can be bland, and that doesn't interest me. But this does. Thyme and lemon elevate the rice. Zucchini gives it a bit of bite. Get someone to help out with making and eating it.

Directions

1. Bring the stock to a boil in a large pan, then reduce to a low simmer.

2. In another pan, melt the butter over low heat. Add the onion, garlic, and thyme. Cook gently for 3 to 5 minutes until soft without coloring.

3. Increase heat. Add the rice. Stir to coat. Tip in the wine, apple juice, or cider and let it bubble. Stir it frequently until half the liquid is gone.

4. Reduce heat. Add 2 ladles of stock. Stir as the rice absorbs it. Add another couple of ladles of stock and stir again till absorbed. Add the turmeric or saffron.

5. Throw in the zucchini, then 2 more ladles of stock and a good squeeze of lemon.

6. Continue stirring and adding stock until you have a creamy, soupy mix. Add more stock if you need to. Don't rush the process—it could take up to 30 minutes. Put some music on and take it easy.

7. Throw in a handful of Parmesan. Season with salt and pepper. Add extra butter if you like.

8. Serve in bowls with extra herbs on top, if desired, and more Parmesan. Pair with endive & watercress salad.

Serves 4
Ingredients
4¼ cups veg or chicken stock (page 138)
4 tablespoons butter
1 medium onion, finely chopped
2 cloves garlic, sliced
2 sprigs fresh thyme
1 cup Arborio or risotto rice
⅓ cup white wine, apple juice, or cider
Small pinch of turmeric, or a few strands of saffron dissolved in 1 tablespoon hot water
1 large zucchini in small cubes (2¼ cups)
¼ lemon
Freshly grated Parmesan
Salt and pepper
Extra butter and herbs (optional)

Eat with: Endive & watercress salad
Toss chopped endive, watercress, and shallot into a bowl. Mix with mustard or other dressing (see page 140 for ideas).

Why Not?
Use local asparagus instead of zucchini when in season (mid-April to late June).

Beans & Peas with Lemon Dressing

Serves 6 to 8
Ingredients
1 pound (2 cups) fresh
  mixed beans & peas,
  including green beans,
  sugar snap peas, and/or
  shelled peas
2 tablespoons chopped
  fresh parsley
2 shallots, thinly sliced
Lemon dressing
1 tablespoon Dijon mustard
Good pinch of sugar
Juice of 1 lemon
4 tablespoons olive oil
3 tablespoons sour cream
  or crème fraîche
Pinch of salt
1 tablespoon hot water

Eat with:
A banquet of salads

Beans and peas get all mixed up in a beautiful little lemon sauce. Best homegrown and in season (summer), though the dressing cheers them up anytime.

Directions
1. Put a large-ish pan one-third full of lightly salted water on to boil.
2. Slide the mix of beans and sugar snap peas in. Boil for 2 minutes.
3. Add the shelled peas. Cook for another 2 minutes or till tender but still crisp to the bite.
4. Meanwhile, fill a bowl with very cold water and a cube or two of ice.
5. Drain the beans and peas and slap them into the ice-cold water to stop the cooking and preserve the color.
6. Drain well. Blot on paper towels if you like. Slap the mixture into a bowl.
7. Stick the dressing ingredients into a jar. Put the lid on and shake well. Alternatively, mix the ingredients in a bowl.
8. Pour the dressing over the beans and peas. Add the parsley and shallots. Mix well. Cool for cookouts.

Spinach, Avocado, & Bacon Salad

Rock 'n' roll with this simple salad. It's a little bit crunchy . . . a little bit salty. Toss in a sharp-suited dressing of your choosing. Coat the salad leaves all over by using your fingers to mix in the dressing.

Serves 2
Ingredients
1 tablespoon olive oil
4 slices bacon
2 slices crustless bread, cubed
Avocado, peeled and cubed
Bunch of baby spinach

Directions
1. Heat the olive oil in a pan. Fry the bacon till crisp. Set on paper towels.
2. Fry the cubes of bread in the bacon fat. Drain on paper towels.
3. Toss the avocado and spinach in a dressing of your choice (see page 140 for ideas). Chop up the bacon.
4. Add the bacon and croutons and toss.

Why Not?
Slap in cooked green beans and a bit of chopped shallot.

Brilliant Vegetables

Bad-guy vegetables turned into heroes. Don't judge them. Just try them.

Slim Sesame Broccoli

Tender broccoli sweetens up in oyster sauce. Slice these guys up for an awesome stir-fry.

Serves 3 to 4
Ingredients
2 teaspoons sesame oil or
  1 tablespoon sunflower oil
2 cloves garlic, thinly sliced
A little fresh ginger, grated
  or sliced
7 ounces (3 cups) broccoli
  florets in ½-inch slices
4 tablespoons stock
  (page 138) or water
2 splashes soy sauce
2 to 3 tablespoons oyster
  sauce

Directions

1. Heat a wok or pan. Add the sesame or sunflower oil.
2. When hot, add the garlic and ginger. Stir quickly to prevent burning.
3. After a few seconds, add the broccoli. Toss and turn for 2 to 3 minutes.
4. Add the stock or water. Stir for another minute or so till just soft with a bit of bite or however you like it. Mix in the soy and oyster sauces.

| **Variation** |
| CHOICE STIR-FRY Try with sliced bok choy or zucchini. |

Fat Broccoli

Tastes a bit like Chinese-restaurant seaweed. Get it nice and dry before you fry it.

Serves 3 to 4
Ingredients
2 big heads of broccoli
2 to 3 tablespoons olive oil
Sea salt
1 lemon, in wedges

Directions

1. Wash the broccoli. Slice very thinly. Slap on a tea towel or paper towel to dry thoroughly.
2. Heat a lidded sauté pan. Add the olive oil.
3. Tip the broccoli in. Slam the lid on.
4. Cook for 2 minutes or till just browned a bit, softening but still crisp. Stir. Replace the lid and cook for another minute.
5. Serve with sea salt and lemon chunks for squeezing.

| **Variation** |
| HOT BROCCOLI Sprinkle with a little de-seeded, finely chopped chili pepper. |

Carrot Pasta

Delicious pasta look-alikes.

Directions

1. Using a potato peeler, cut the carrots into ribbons.
2. Slap the carrots into a pot of boiling water for 20 seconds. Drain.
3. Melt the butter and sugar in a pan. When hot, toss in the carrots.
4. Stir-fry for 2 to 3 minutes till just soft. Add the lemon or lime rind and season. Mix some herbs in.

Serves 3 to 4
Ingredients
4 carrots, peeled
2 tablespoons butter
1 tablespoon sugar
Rind of ½ lemon or 1 lime, grated
Salt and pepper to taste
Sprinkle of thyme or finely chopped fresh sage, parsley, or rosemary

Edgy Cumin Cauliflower

Dress up your cauliflower. This veg needs it.

Directions

1. Preheat oven to 425°F.
2. Tip the cauli onto a baking sheet. Add the garlic, drizzle with a little oil, and sprinkle with cumin and sea salt to taste. Turn to coat.
3. Roast till tender. Delicious hot or cold.

Serves 3 to 4
Ingredients
1 cauliflower, cut in small florets
3 cloves garlic, peeled and sliced
Olive oil
Ground cumin
Coarse sea salt

Meat

Andy's goal-orientated, so he went straight for meat. Steak's his meal of choice—at school, sometimes he goes off to our friendly neighborhood butcher, then back to the common-room kitchen for a bit of indoor grilling. My challenge? Get him to diversify and tackle other kinds of lovely stuff, like my roast crunchy duck, glazed ham, top sausage Yorkshires, lamb or chicken korma, lovely lamb koftas, plus some of the leaner eats you can do with chicken. Meat's major protein. Eat it to power yourself on. And red meat's great for sharpening the brain—it's the iron. Get yourself loads of veg, salad, and carbs with it. Buying your own meat? Try to get free-range and local if you can. Proper butchers know how to treat it so you'll get more interesting cuts and a better flavor. Andy's family gets theirs from the market. Cook it in a variety of ways—roasting, grilling, baking, boiling. Occasionally fry it, but if you want to stay on the ball, keep the fat down.

Top Sausage Yorkshires

Makes 8
Ingredients
4 eggs
1¼ cups milk
Pinch of salt
8 Italian sausages
Sunflower or light olive oil
1¾ cups flour
Pepper

Variations
BACON & HERB
At STEP 3, stretch 4 slices of bacon until thin. Cut in half. Wrap each half around a sausage. Tuck a sprig of rosemary in between if you like.
VEGETARIAN
At STEP 3, lightly fry vegetarian sausages or throw in some roasted butternut squash and red onion.
CLASSIC TOAD IN THE HOLE
At STEP 3, put 6 to 8 large sausages into a large baking pan (12 x 8 x 3 inches) with a bit of oil. Bake for 6 minutes. Skip STEP 4, and at STEP 6, while the oil in the pan is still very hot, pour the batter mix over it. Cook for 20 to 40 minutes.

Why Not?
Try using big sausages. Or make plain without sausages.

Classic toad-in-the-hole, but easier and speedier. Crispy, golden, and packed with a sausage. Slap in the oven after the game. Team with creamy mash, onion relish, and homestyle ketchup.

Directions
1. Preheat oven to 450°F.
2. Whisk the eggs and milk together with a pinch of salt using an electric mixer (whisk attachment) or by hand with a balloon or electric hand whisk till it looks like a milk shake. Leave for 20 minutes.
3. Set the sausages on a baking sheet. Bake for 5 minutes.
4. Drizzle a bit of oil into eight holes of a large muffin pan. Put in the oven to preheat. The hotter they are, the higher the batter will rise.
5. Sift the flour and pepper into the milk. Whisk furiously by hand or machine. Tip into a measuring jug.
6. Remove the sizzling pan from the oven. Set a sausage in each hole. Pour the batter in right up to the rims.
7. Slide the pan carefully back onto the middle shelf to rise. Cook without opening the door for 20 minutes till the Yorkshires are high and golden.

Korma & Cucumber Salad

Every week the lads either head off for a curry or make an awesome one at home. Korma's a brilliant match of spices, almonds, and yogurt that doesn't pack too much heat. Give it a try with cooling cucumber salad.

Directions

1. Slap the lamb or chicken in a bowl with half the yogurt. Mix to coat.
2. Tip onion, chili pepper, garlic, ginger, almonds, korma paste, water, and half the cilantro into a blender or processor. Blitz to a fine paste. (By hand: chop fine and stir in the water.)
3. Tip the oil into a large pan over low heat. Add the mixture. Stir for 1 minute to stop it from sticking as it thickens.
4. Chuck the lamb or chicken in with the salt and lemon juice. Mix well.
5. Increase heat to bring curry to a gentle boil, stirring.
6. Reduce to very low heat. Cook, covered, for 1 hour. Occasionally check. Add a splash of water if it gets too dry, but you want a thick sauce.
7. Add the remaining yogurt. Cook for a further 30 to 40 minutes. (You can also cook this in the oven at 400°F for 20 mintues, then lower heat slightly for 1 hour or till tender.) Meanwhile, make the cucumber salad.
8. Taste the korma. Adjust seasoning, adding more lemon juice or yogurt. Serve over rice with the cucumber salad on top. Enjoy.

Serves 4
Ingredients
2 pounds cubed lamb or chicken
4 tablespoons plain yogurt
2 onions, chopped
2 chili peppers, de-seeded and chopped
2 cloves garlic, chopped
1-inch piece of ginger, peeled and grated
½ cup ground almonds
4 tablespoons korma paste
½ cup water
Handful of fresh cilantro
2 tablespoons peanut or sunflower oil
Pinch of salt
Squeeze of lemon juice

Cucumber salad
1 cucumber
1 teaspoon salt
1 tablespoon plain yogurt
2 tablespoons creamed coconut
1 clove garlic, crushed
1 to 2 chili peppers, de-seeded and finely sliced
1 small onion, thinly sliced
2 tablespoons lime juice

Peel the cucumber and slice it in half lengthwise. Whip the seeds out with a teaspoon. Cut the flesh across in thin half-moon shapes. Sprinkle with the salt and leave for 30 minutes. Rinse and dry. Combine all the other salad ingredients. Mix in the cucumber.

Eat with:
Basmati rice (page 84)
Poppadoms
Warm naan bread
Mango chutney

Why Not?
Make korma a day or two ahead to save time and develop flavor.

Glazed Ham & Pease Pudding

Serves 6
Ingredients
4½-pound ham joint
2 bay leaves
Peeled onion
8 black peppercorns
2 tablespoons maple syrup
  or brown sugar
Whole cloves
Glaze
1 cup brown sugar
1-inch piece peeled ginger,
  grated
2 tablespoons English
  mustard
Juice of 1 lemon
3 tablespoons apple juice
  or water

Pease pudding
1 cup yellow split peas,
  soaked overnight
1 small carrot, chopped
1 small onion, chopped
2 cloves garlic, crushed
1 bay leaf
Stock from ham or water
Butter
Salt and pepper
Grated nutmeg

Eat with:
Mash (page 22)
Baked spuds (page 98)
Roast potatoes
Crunchy herb spuds
  (page 99)
Red cabbage (page 67)
Coleslaw (page 140)
Orange salad (page 140)
Potato salad (page 96)
Applesauce (page 138)

If you're a ham fan, you'll love this. The sugar glaze packs the meat with taste and looks magnificent. Eat some hot. Save the rest for salads, sandwiches, and teaming up with other stuff. One bit of cooking makes a week of eating.

Directions

1. Day or two before: Tie the joint with string like a parcel to keep it together. Put it into a large bowl. Cover with cold water to draw out the salt. Fridge it.
2. On the day: Drain. Put the meat into a very large pan or casserole dish. Cover with fresh water. Add the bay leaves, onion, peppercorns, and syrup or sugar.
3. Set the pan on a low heat. Bring to a boil very slowly (could take 30 minutes).
4. Reduce heat, simmer gently for 45 minutes, then remove.
5. Pease pudding: Drain the soaked split peas. Slap in a pan with the carrot, onion, garlic, bay leaf, and stock or water. Boil fiercely for at least 10 minutes. Cover. Simmer over low heat for 1 to 1½ hours till tender.
6. Whisk the glaze ingredients together in a pan over low heat with a balloon whisk. Boil for a few minutes to reduce to a syrup. Set aside.
7. Preheat oven to 400°F.
8. Drain the meat over a bowl (save the liquid for stock). Chuck out the onion, etc.
9. Set the meat on a board. Cut the skin away from the top, leaving the fat. Score a crisscross pattern across the top of the ham, but don't cut the string. Stick whole cloves in.
10. Set the meat in a roasting pan. Brush with the glaze. Cook for 30 to 45 minutes, re-glazing 4 times to flavor and color. Rest the meat for at least 10 minutes before carving.
11. Drain the peas. Bash up with butter, salt and pepper, and some nutmeg, using a masher.

Crunchy Chicken Strips

Serves 4
Ingredients
4 chicken breasts
Butter and oil for frying
White flour for coating
3 good pinches chili powder
Salt and pepper
1 to 2 eggs, beaten
Polenta or cornmeal

Eat with:
Salsa verde
3 crushed garlic cloves
1 bunch parsley, torn
1 bunch basil, torn
1½ tablespoons rinsed
    capers
1 tablespoon Dijon mustard
1 tablespoon white wine
    vinegar
6 to 8 tablespoons extra-
    virgin olive oil

Add the ingredients to a food processor to mix while slowly drizzling in olive oil till you get a mayo-style mix. Store in the fridge and stir before serving.

Dips
Sweet chili sauce
Mustard or hot mayo
    (page 139)
Homestyle ketchup
    (page 139)

They're tasty. Polenta gets chicken excellently crunchy. Perfect for supper with dips and fat fries. Prep loads ahead to whack into baskets for party-style munchies.

Directions
1. Make salsa verde.
2. Preheat oven to 400°F. Flatten the chicken filets. Lay on a board between plastic wrap. Bash with the flat of your hand or a rolling pin.
3. Cut the chicken into slices—at least 3 inches or longer.
4. Slap the flour, chili powder, salt and pepper onto one large plate. Put the beaten eggs on a second. Spread the polenta or cornmeal onto a third. Coat the chicken slices in flour, egg, then polenta or cornmeal. Set on a baking sheet.
5. Cook for 10 minutes till white all through (stick a knife in to check) or fry for 2 to 3 minutes on each side in a little butter and oil till done.
6. Serve with salsa verde, oven fries (page 32), or a salad.

Ingredients
4 skinless chicken breasts
Marinade
2-inch piece ginger, peeled
   and grated
Rind of 2 plump limes and
   juice of 4 plump limes
1 clove garlic, crushed
3 tablespoons finely
   chopped cilantro
Olive oil
Sea salt

Lime Chicken

I adore this. I've almost eaten it too often, it's so addictive. Marinate the chicken in the fridge overnight to maximize taste and save time. It's light (good for health and weight) and packed with useful protein for a training boost.

Directions

1. Flatten the chicken a bit using the flat of your hand or lay between plastic wrap and bash with a rolling pin.
2. Mix the ginger, lime rind and juice, garlic, cilantro, and a good glug of olive oil. Save half for dressing.
3. Tip the rest into a shallow dish. Add in the chicken. Coat it well in the marinade. Leave for at least 30 minutes but longer if you like. Wash your hands well after handling the raw chicken.
4. Put a lightly oiled grill or frying pan on to heat. Slap the chicken on to sizzle. Turn when the first side is browned. Cook the other side. Turn again if you need to. Cooking time will vary depending on the thickness of the meat and the degree of heat. Each filet should be cooked through (white) but still moist. Test it with a knife to check. Season with sea salt.
5. Serve the chicken in one piece or cut into diagonals. Add a bit more oil to the reserved dressing and drizzle it all over. Set on rice or couscous. Also great with crispy herbed spuds, salad, or grilled veg, e.g., zucchini, eggplant, or butternut squash. Tasty!

Variations
LIME KEBABS
At STEP 1, leave the chicken unflattened. Cut it into chunks. At STEP 4, preheat grill. Thread the chicken onto metal skewers or wooden ones soaked in cold water for 20 minutes. Grill, turning till done. Serve with veg.
VEGGIE
Use tofu instead of chicken.
THAI CHICKEN FINGERS
At STEP 1, cut the chicken into thin finger-length strips. At STEP 2, put the dressing ingredients into a blender, adding 1 chopped red chili pepper. Use lemons instead of limes and mint instead of cilantro if you like. Spicy. Delicious.

Why Not?
Chop lime chicken into a wrap or salad for a lean eat or snack.

Roast Pork with Apples & Trimmings

This one's asking to be Sunday lunch, though it's easy enough to work it in midweek. Chuck your apples in to bake with the meat. It flavors up the spuds. Makes a nice fruity gravy.

Directions

1. Boil the spuds in a large pan of lightly salted water for 5 to 10 minutes till just softening. Drain well. Set aside.

2. Preheat oven to 400°F.

3. Score the rind of the pork loin. Cut close parallel lines across the skin on the meat with a sharp knife, leaving any string intact.

4. Rub sea salt into the lines and the top. Stick herb sprigs in.

5. Put a good glug of oil in a large roasting pan. Set the meat in there. Roast for 10 minutes, then stick the spuds in, turning them in the sizzling fat. Roast for another 10 minutes.

6. Reduce heat to 375°F. Set the apples cut-side down in the pan with the garlic cloves.

7. Cook till the meat is done. (Depends on joint size. Test by poking with a skewer. Juices should run clear and meat should be cooked through.) Rest in a warm place. Remove the apples and garlic before they fall apart.

8. Increase heat to 425°F. Move the pan with spuds up a shelf to crisp. Remove and keep warm when done.

9. Gravy: Add a bit of water to the apple-y juices in the pan. Scrape any bits off with a wooden spoon. Stir over the heat to boil.

10. Carve the meat. Give everyone potatoes, apple, garlic, and gravy.

Serves 4

Ingredients

4 large potatoes (Yukon Gold or russet are good), peeled and quartered
1 small pork loin with bone
Coarse sea salt
4 to 6 bits of rosemary or sage
Olive or sunflower oil
2 apples, halved
6 to 8 cloves garlic

Eat with:

Green-bean spaghetti (page 53)
Baked cauliflower (page 73)
Carrot pasta (page 73)

Variation

CRACKLING
Preheat oven to 425°F. Cut the skin off the pork with a sharp knife. Set in a pan. Salt it. Roast for 40 minutes or till crisp. Keep warm. Reduce heat to 400°F. Smear a honey and mustard mix over the fat on the pork loin joint and roast as in recipe. Eat with the crackling.

Why Not?

Make yourself a lovely hot pork roll. Slap a slice between bread with mustard and warm applesauce. Or try it cold with applesauce, mustard mayo (page 139), arugula, and coleslaw.

Perfect Beef Stir-Fry

Serves 2 to 3
Ingredients
Marinade
1 pound rump or sirloin
steak
3 cloves garlic, peeled and
finely chopped
1 teaspoon finely chopped
cilantro
2 tablespoons soy sauce
1 tablespoon rice wine
2 teaspoons sugar
1 tablespoon cornstarch
Rice
¾ cup basmati rice
1½ cups cold water
Sauce
2 tablespoons soy sauce
1½ teaspoons sugar
Squeeze of lime (optional)
Dash of sesame oil
Stir-fry
2 tablespoons sunflower oil
1 teaspoon sesame oil
6 green onions, chopped
lengthwise

Variations
DUCK STIR-FRY
Use sliced duck
breasts (fat removed)
instead of beef.
VEGGIE STIR-FRY
Use mushrooms or
tofu.

Stir-fries can be a bit average, but I've never complained about this one. All the oriental flavors complement one another beautifully to produce a really awesome dish.

Directions
1. Cut the beef into thin diagonal slices across the grain. Slice into bite-size bits.
2. Slap in a bowl with the garlic, cilantro, soy sauce, rice wine, sugar, and cornstarch. Marinate for 30 minutes or more (fridge overnight if you'd like).
3. Wash the rice in a strainer. Add to a pan with the water. Bring to a boil. Cover. Simmer on low heat for 10 minutes or till water is absorbed. Remove.
4. Meanwhile, mix the sauce ingredients together.
5. Heat a wok or deep frying pan. Add the sunflower and sesame oils. Chuck in half the beef. Stir-fry for 1 to 2 minutes using a long-handled wooden spoon till just browned. (Don't overcook. Gets leathery.) Remove. Keep warm. Repeat with the rest of beef. Remove.
6. Stir-fry the green onions for 1 minute. Slap the beef back in to reheat. Add the sauce. Stir well to heat through.
7. Drain the rice. Fluff with a fork. Stuff into bowls. Top with the stir-fry.

Steak Jalapeño Pockets

These can be absolutely packed and massive, as I found out to my messy delight—bits of marinated steak and filling flying everywhere—or make yours trim and neat. Your choice.

Directions

1. Smash the garlic, peppers, coriander, salt, and pepper together with a pestle and mortar. Tip into a jar or container. Add the lime and lemon juices, vinegar, and oil. Screw the lid on and shake.

2. Slap the steaks into a shallow dish. Tip the marinade over. Rub in well. Chill for at least 1 hour. Return to room temperature before cooking.

3. Prepare fillings of your choice just before cooking the meat.

4. Get your grill or frying pan hot. Slap the steaks on. Cook for 2 minutes per side or till done as you like. Beef's best when still pink inside. Rest the meat somewhere warm.

5. Warm the tortillas in a frying pan or oven till soft.

6. Carve the meat into thin diagonals. Chuck into the tortillas with the fillings.

Serves 4
Ingredients
4 rump or sirloin steaks
8 tortilla wraps
Marinade
4 cloves garlic, peeled and crushed
4 to 6 pickled jalapeño peppers, chopped
2 tablespoons coriander
Sea salt and pepper
Juice of 2 limes
Juice of 1 lemon
1 tablespoon white wine vinegar
2 tablespoons olive oil
Fillings
Guacamole (page 139)
Sour cream
Chopped tomato or salsa (page 140)
Iceberg or other crisp lettuce
Chopped red onion
Grated Cheddar

Variation
CHICKEN POCKETS
At STEP 2, flatten 4 chicken filets with a rolling pin. Slap them into the marinade. At STEP 4, cook for 5 minutes on each side or till white and tender. Eat hot as above or cold in a wrap, salad, or sandwich.

Whole Roast Crunchy Duck & Sauce

Serves 3 to 4
Ingredients
1 duck, approximately 6
   pounds
Sea salt and pepper

Cherry sauce
Slap 3 to 4 tablespoons
cherry jam into a pan with
$2/3$ cup red wine or
pomegranate juice. Whisk.
Simmer gently for 5
minutes.

Marmalade sauce
Whack 3 to 4 tablespoons
marmalade into a pan with
the juice of a large orange
or $2/3$ cup orange juice or
ginger ale. Whisk. Simmer
gently for 5 minutes.

Eat with:
Spuds roasted in duck fat
Boiled baby spuds rolled in
   parsley or mint, butter,
   salt, lemon, and pepper
Watercress

Why Not?
Use leftover duck in a
wrap. Shred and mix
with matchstick-cut
cucumber, green onion,
and a bit of cherry jam
or hoisin sauce.

I've been known to polish off half a duck myself. This is a
top family favorite. It's so easy and looks so good. Serve
with a fruity sauce. Save the fat for roasting potatoes.

Directions
1. Preheat oven to 425°F.
2. Dry the duck with paper towels (a dry duck is a crispy duck).
3. Set it on a rack in a roasting pan.
4. Prick the skin all over with a fork. Rub in sea salt and pepper to taste.
5. Roast for 25 minutes. Pour the fat off carefully into a bowl.
6. Decrease temperature to 350°F.
7. Leave the duck to cook for 2 hours. Carefully pour off the fat every 30
minutes or so.
8. Meanwhile, make your sauce of choice.
9. Let the duck rest for 5 minutes when it's done (deep golden brown, salty, and crispy).
10. Cut into 4 parts with a sharp knife, kitchen shears, or scissors. Cut along the back to get it in half, then just above the leg to quarter it. Plate it. Tip the sauce over it.

Sweet Five-Spice Duck Legs

A personal favorite. I love my duck to have a crispy skin, and the five-spice powder adds cool Asian flavor. The sauce is essential. Rest these guys on a pile of fried potatoes and enjoy with a mountain of salad. Makes a great treat to impress someone special.

Directions

1. Preheat oven to 400°F.
2. Chuck the duck or chicken legs into a roasting pan or dish big enough to fit them in a single layer. Lay the rosemary and garlic cloves underneath.
3. Prick the legs all over with a fork. Rub a mix of five-spice powder and sea salt into the skin. Bake for 1 hour. Pour fat off carefully once or twice.
4. Meanwhile, melt the red currant jelly or cherry jam with the wine or juice and water in a small pan. Use a balloon whisk to break up the jelly. Simmer it for 5 minutes or till well amalgamated. Remove from heat.
5. Remove the duck. Pour off the remaining fat. Tip the liquid jelly over the meat. Roast for another 15 minutes. Cracking.

Serves 4
Ingredients
4 duck or chicken legs
2 sprigs rosemary
4 cloves garlic, peeled
1 to 2 teaspoons Chinese
   five-spice powder
1 to 2 teaspoons sea salt
2 tablespoons red currant
   jelly or cherry jam
2/3 cup red wine, apple juice,
   or pomegranate juice
4 tablespoons water

Eat with:
Crunchy herb spuds (page
   99) or mash (page 22)
Green-bean spaghetti
   (page 53) or peas
Butternut squash

Why Not?
Try roast duck breast. Fry duck-breast filets till brown on each side. Roast on a rack at 425°F for 10 minutes or till done as you like. Rest for 3 minutes. Slice diagonally. Drizzle with a little pomegranate juice and molasses. It fizzes!

Hot Dogs & Relish

Makes 6 to 8

Ingredients

1½ pounds pork steak, shoulder or ground pork
2 to 3 teaspoons fennel seeds
⅓ cup breadcrumbs
3 cloves garlic, crushed
1 to 2 red chili peppers, de-seeded and finely chopped
3 green onions
Grated lemon rind
Salt and pepper
Olive oil for cooking
8 rolls or buns

Relish

1 tablespoon olive oil
1 tablespoon butter
2 big red onions, thinly sliced
½ to 1 tablespoon brown sugar
2 tablespoons balsamic vinegar

Variations

HOMESTYLE PORK BURGERS

At STEP 1, blitz coarser mince than for sausages. At STEP 6, mold into burger shapes. At STEP 7, fry or grill the burgers. At STEP 8, stack with tomato, arugula, sliced Gruyère, and cooked apple or pineapple.

PORK & FENNEL MEATBALLS

At STEP 6, roll the mix into meatballs. Fry to color. Set the balls in my tomato-ginger sauce (page 52). Simmer gently in a covered pan for 10 to 15 minutes or till cooked through. Set on a heap of spaghetti or penne. Sprinkle with Parmesan.

Why Not?

Skip the bun. Enjoy with mash 'n' onion gravy, or slap 'em on couscous.

Way healthier than bought hot dogs, these also taste so much better—a winning combo. Fennel's a great flavorer of pork, but use your own herb or spice if you like. You've got to try the sweet onion relish—it's brilliant.

Directions

1. If making your own mince, cut the meat into cubes. Blitz a few at a time in a processor for a coarse sausage-style paste. If using ground pork, blitz it in a processor to make it pastier.

2. Crush the fennel roughly in a pestle and mortar for bits, or blitz to a powder in a spice or coffee grinder.

3. Slap the mince, breadcrumbs, fennel, garlic, chili pepper, finely chopped green onion, lemon rind, salt, and pepper into a bowl. Mix with your hands, squeezing the ingredients together. Chill for 30 minutes or more.

4. Relish: Heat the oil and butter in a pan. Cook the onion over very low heat for 10 minutes till softened but not colored.

5. Stir in the sugar and vinegar. Cook gently for 20 minutes till sticky and jamlike.

6. Shape the pork mix into 6 to 8 sausages, squeezing together. Brush with olive oil.

7. Heat a bit of oil in a frying pan. Fry the sausages gently on all sides. If a bit breaks off, don't panic. Cook all through or fry to brown all sides, then cook at 400°F for 10 minutes or till cooked through.

8. Slap into a roll or bun with the onion relish, ketchup (page 139), mustard, and salad leaves.

Lovely Lamb Koftas

Makes 8
Ingredients
1½ pounds ground lamb
2 small onions, grated
4 cloves garlic, crushed
1 teaspoon allspice
½ teaspoon ground cumin
¼ teaspoon sweet paprika
1 teaspoon dried chili flakes
3 tablespoons chopped flat-
   leaf parsley
Salt and pepper
Sunflower oil for brushing

Eat with:
Baba ghanoush
Preheat oven to 400°F.
Roast 2 eggplants on a
baking sheet till the skin
blackens and flesh softens (30
to 45 minutes). Cool. Peel
the skin away. Drain in a
colander for 30 minutes. Blitz
in a blender or processor
with 2 crushed garlic cloves.
Mix in 2 tablespoons tahini,
3 tablespoons lemon juice,
½ teaspoon ground cumin,
and sea salt to taste. Sprinkle
with chopped parsley. Chill.

Variation
KOFTA POCKETS
At STEP 1, cover 5
ounces bulgur wheat
with boiling water. Soak
for 30 minutes. Drain
and dry. At STEP 2,
add the dried soaked
wheat to the lamb mix.
At STEP 3, divide into
burger shapes, but do
not squeeze. At STEP
6, fry for 4 minutes on
each side or till cooked
through. Slap in a pita
with hummus, garlic,

Juicy lamb on sticks with loads of warm spices. Get the best mince, or mince your own lamb in a processor. Wraparound kebabs, basically. Team with baba

Directions
1. If using wooden skewers, soak them in cold water for 20 minutes before you cook.
2. Slap the lamb into a bowl with the grated onion, garlic, spices, chili, parsley, salt, and pepper. Add a splash of water to bind.
3. Mix together with your hands, squeezing the components together into a smooth paste. Divide the paste into 8 fat sausage shapes.
4. Chill for later, or if cooking now, preheat the grill or frying pan.
5. Take a metal or wooden skewer. Thread a sausage, then elongate and mold it around the skewer for a thinner sausage. Repeat.
6. Brush each sausage with a little oil. Grill or fry the meat, turning as you go, till cooked through (5 to 10 minutes). Serve with baba ghanoush, warm pitas, tzatziki, hummus, rice or couscous, and tomato & onion salad (page 141).

Chicken in a Paper Bag

For very little effort, you get a fabulous Chinese meal. Baking it in the bag makes the meat extra tender.

Directions

1. Mix the hoisin sauce, garlic (if using), cooking wine, and oil in a bowl. Chuck in the chicken. Mix well. Leave for at least 30 minutes to marinate.
2. Add the green onion. Preheat oven to 400°F.
3. Cut out two large squares of parchment paper. Divide the chicken mix between them, setting it in a single layer. Make two parcels. Scrunch or fold the paper up, enclosing the meat but leaving room for the steam to rise. Set the parcels on a baking sheet. Cook for 20 minutes.
4. Meanwhile, prepare your rice. Wash in a strainer under the tap. Slap in a pan with the water. Bring to a boil. Cover. Simmer on low heat for 10 minutes or till the water's absorbed. Take from heat and let it stand.
5. **Stir-fry:** Heat a wok and add the oils, garlic, and green onion and fry till soft. Chuck in the ginger, if using, and the bok choy. Stir-fry till tender. Add the soy sauce, rice wine, and sugar. Heat through.
6. Test to see if the chicken is cooked—all white (no pink).
7. Drain and fluff the rice with a fork. Serve in bowls with the stir-fry and top with the chicken.

Serves 2
Ingredients
Marinade
2 to 3 tablespoons hoisin sauce
1 clove garlic, crushed (optional)
A little Chinese cooking wine
Drizzle of sesame oil
2 green onions, sliced
Chicken
2 large chicken breasts, cut in bite-size pieces
Rice
½ cup rice
⅔ cup cold water
Stir-fry
2 teaspoons sesame oil
1 tablespoon sunflower oil
2 cloves garlic, crushed
1 bunch green onion, chopped
2 to 3 gratings fresh ginger (optional)
3 bunches bok choy, chopped
Splash of soy sauce
Splash of Chinese rice wine
Good pinch of sugar

Why Not?

Unwrap the parcels. Tip onto a bed of stir-fried noodles and bok choy.

Potatoes

Liv's passionate about spuds. Weird, I know, but I'm with her all the way. There's nothing like a properly cooked potato. Picking the right type is particularly important for cooking. You've got to cast them correctly. Floury characters (Yukon Gold and russet) are real heroes and like to be mashed (Liv's favorite), bashed, roasted, fried, and smashed up for potato cakes. Waxy salad spuds prefer sharp action—slicing and chopping for salads, hash, bravas, frittatas. Don't imagine that potatoes are just there for their carbs, by the way. You can turn that beautiful energy into really cool food, like fine potato pancakes to dish up with home-cured salmon. Friends over for dinner? Whip up some sweet-potato gnocchi. Favorites like old-school Cornish pasties and luscious shepherd's pie rely on good winter potatoes. In the summertime, get new ones—light and lovely with a bit of butter, seasoning, fresh herbs, and lemon. OK, grocery stores break all the rules so that we can have new potatoes in December—but they just don't look right with Christmas dinner. Spuds are great comfort food.

Neat Potato Cakes

Makes 8
Ingredients
1½ pounds floury potatoes, peeled
2 tablespoons butter
1 egg yolk
1 teaspoon mustard
Squeeze of lemon juice
Salt and pepper
Flour for coating
Olive or sunflower oil and butter or duck fat

Eat with:
Sausages—good ones baked in the oven till brown and cooked through
Fish—a pile of roughly chopped smoked salmon, cherry tomato, dill, and olives in a bit of sour cream and horseradish
Eggs—fried in olive oil
Bacon—crisply fried
Ham—cold sliced

Variations
At STEP 4, add for:
FISH CAKES
Flaked cooked salmon
BACON CAKES
Crisply cooked bacon
CHEESE CAKES
Handful of grated Cheddar or Gruyère
MUSHROOM CAKES
Lightly fried mushrooms
BUBBLE & SQUEAK
Cooked bacon and shredded cabbage
HERB CAKES
Finely chopped fresh dill, parsley, or cilantro

They're not posh, but so what? Potato cakes work brilliantly alongside other food favorites (sausages, steaks, fish, veggie stews) and easily adapt to star on their own (fish cakes, bacon cakes, cheese cakes). Season well to maximize flavor.

Directions

1. Bring a large pan of lightly salted water to a boil.
2. Cut the potatoes into large chunks. Boil until just tender.
3. Drain. Slap back into the warm pan. Jiggle for 1 minute to dry.
4. Mash well with a fork or masher. Add the butter, egg yolk, mustard, lemon juice, salt, and pepper. Beat together till stiffly creamy.
5. Scatter the flour over a large plate. Season lightly.
6. Flour your hands a bit. Divide the

mash and shape into 8 flattish cakes. Dip each one into the flour, shaking off excess. Chill, or cook now.
7. Heat the oil and butter or duck fat till hot in a large pan. Fry the cakes for 5 minutes on each side till hot through and golden (don't flip too soon or they'll stick), or heat in the oven on a baking sheet for 10 to 15 minutes at 375°F. Turn. Bake for another 10 minutes till crisp and tempting.

Sweet-Potato Gnocchi

Italian dumplings or Chinese dim sum? These guys have elements of both (it's the ginger). A perfect dish for a date-style dinner.

Directions

1. Preheat oven to 400°F.

2. Wash the sweet potatoes. Prick with a fork. Slap on a baking sheet and bake for 40 to 60 minutes or till tender. Remove. Slice in half. Cool for 2 minutes.

3. Scoop the flesh out into a clean tea towel or a bit of muslin. Twist to enclose it. Squeeze to remove excess moisture. Scrape into a bowl.

4. Add the ginger, salt, pepper, egg yolk, and Parmesan. Sift in the flour. Mix together with a fork and fingers for a soft, warm dough, but handle very lightly.

5. Cut into 4 pieces on a lightly floured board. Cover 3 with a cloth. Roll the first piece into a long, thin sausage. Cut into 10 pieces. Cover. Repeat with the 3 remaining pieces.

6. Put a large pan of lightly salted water on to boil. Slip the gnocchi carefully in. Boil for 2 minutes or till they rise. Remove with a slotted spoon. Drain. Slap into a bowl with a tiny bit of olive oil.

7. Melt the butter in a small pan. Add the garlic, lemon, and herbs. Pour over the gnocchi.

Serves 3 to 4

Ingredients

¾ pound sweet potatoes in skins
Small piece of peeled fresh ginger, very finely grated
Salt and pepper
1 egg yolk
1 tablespoon grated Parmesan
1¼ cups white flour
Olive oil

Sauce

4 tablespoons butter
2 cloves garlic, crushed
Good squeeze of lemon juice
Any herbs

Eat with:

Warm bread to mop up juices
Arugula
Freshly grated Parmesan

Two Mean Potato Salads

Serves 4
Ingredients

1½ pounds old potatoes, peeled, or new potatoes, unpeeled, chopped into large chunks

4 to 6 cloves garlic with skins left on

2 to 3 tablespoons mayonnaise

2 to 3 tablespoons plain yogurt or sour cream

Squeeze of lemon juice

Handful of fresh parsley, dill, or cilantro, finely chopped

Salt and pepper

Variation

TANGY POTATO SALAD

At STEP 3, add slices of red onion, chopped baby pickles, and cherry tomatoes.

Serves 4
Ingredients

1½ pounds old potatoes, peeled, or new potatoes, unpeeled, chopped into large chunks

4 tablespoons mayonnaise

1 to 1½ tablespoons Chinese wine vinegar

2 drops sesame oil

1 clove garlic, crushed

1 to 2 teaspoons horseradish sauce

Squeeze of lemon

Fresh parsley, thyme, or cilantro, finely chopped

Salt and pepper

4 green onions, sliced

6 radishes, finely chopped

½ cucumber, finely sliced

3 slices ham, shredded

Alfalfa sprouts

Creamy Garlic

Mix and match with other salads.

Directions

1. Boil the spuds and garlic in lightly salted water till just tender (test with a knife). If using old, floury ones, watch that they don't disintegrate.

2. Drain. Separate the spuds from the garlic. Cool them a bit.

3. Remove the garlic from the skins. Smush the flesh in a bowl. Mix in the mayo and yogurt or sour cream. Add the lemon juice, herbs, salt, and pepper.

4. Mix into the spuds. Team with any salad or cold meats.

East Meets West

One cultural shock of a fancy salad. Western-style potatoes mix with a Chinese-inspired dressing.

Directions

1. Boil the potatoes in lightly salted water till just tender. Drain and set aside.

2. Meanwhile, mix the mayo, vinegar, sesame oil, garlic, horseradish, lemon juice, herbs, salt, and pepper. Stir in the green onions.

3. When the potatoes are just warm, stir in the mayo mix.

4. Add most of the radish, cucumber, and half the ham. Top with the remaining ham and sprinkle sprouts over it.

5. Cool it. Eat it.

Serves 4
Ingredients
4 large baking potatoes
Sunflower or olive oil
   (optional)
Butter
Lemon juice
Salt and pepper

Variations

GARLIC BUTTER
Mix 2 tablespoons of soft butter with 1 clove crushed garlic, salt, and pepper. Slice the baked spuds in two. Dab a bit of garlic butter over the top of each. Finish under a hot broiler till bubbling.

CRUNCHY MUSTARD
Top baked, halved spuds with a mix of mustard and garlic breadcrumbs (page 47) before grilling.

FILLED SKINS
Bake leftover or scooped-out skins. Brush the insides with butter and seasoning. Add a cheese of your choice. Heat in the hottest oven for 10 minutes or till crisp. Fill with lettuce and guacamole or sour cream mixed with dill and crushed garlic.

ROAST BAKERS
At STEP 6, chop hot baked spuds into large chunks. Slap in a roasting pan. Increase oven heat to maximum. Drizzle with a bit of olive oil, salt, and pepper or paprika. Roast for 15 minutes.

Banging Baked Potatoes

What can I say? Liv's favorite bakers.

Directions
1. Preheat oven to 400°F.
2. Scrub the spuds and set on a baking sheet. Prick with a fork or stick metal skewers through each (cuts cooking time).
3. Crisp: Rub the skins with a bit of oil and salt.
Soft: Wrap in foil or bake as is.
4. Cook for 1 hour or till tender.
5. Slice in two or cut a cross in the top. Mash in your butter, lemon juice, salt, and pepper, and slap on a topping, if you like:
Italian: Ragu (page 55), grated Parmesan
Spicy: Veggie chili (page 65), sour cream, grated Cheddar
Chic: Sour cream and chives with arugula, cherry tomatoes, watercress
Classic: Shredded ham, chopped apple, dates, celery, garlic in sour cream or mayo
Greek: Diced feta, cucumber, tomatoes, black olives
Tex-Mex: Guacamole, grated Cheddar, sour cream, salsa (page 140)

Crunchy Herb Spuds & French Chicken

Get these slow-roasted garlic spuds into your repertoire. They're winners on their own or with just about anything. Love 'em. A luxurious dish to impress friends with.

Directions

1. Preheat oven to 425°F.
2. Cut the potatoes into bite-size chunks. Slap them into a nonstick roasting pan with the garlic and finely chopped rosemary. Drizzle with olive oil. Turn to coat. Roast for 50 to 60 minutes or till crisp outside, tender in the middle. Turn once or twice during cooking.
3. 20 minutes before the spuds are done, put the chicken between 2 layers of plastic wrap. Flatten by bashing with a rolling pin. Don't bother if your filets are already thin.
4. Tip the flour onto a large plate. Season it with salt and pepper. Set the chicken in and turn it to coat well.

5. Put the oil and butter into a large heavy-bottomed frying pan. Heat till it starts to brown, but don't let it burn. Add the chicken. Cook for 3 to 4 minutes or till the bottom browns (check). Turn.
6. Fry for another 5 to 6 minutes or till cooked through (white, not pink). Test by cutting the fattest part. Remove and keep warm.
7. **Sauce:** Pour the wine, juice, or stock into the pan. Stir well to incorporate all the pan bits and juices where the flavor sits. Boil for 2 to 3 minutes till it reduces a bit. Add in the mustard and crème fraîche. Stir. Let it bubble for another 3 minutes.
8. Season the sauce with salt and pepper. Pour over the chicken. Sprinkle with the chopped herbs. Serve with crunchy potatoes and great bread to mop up the juices. Classic.

Serves 4
Ingredients
Potatoes
4 baking potatoes, peeled
8 cloves garlic, chopped
3 sprigs rosemary
Olive oil
Chicken
4 chicken breasts
Flour for coating
Salt and pepper
1 tablespoon olive oil
1 tablespoon butter
Sauce
⅔ cup white wine, apple juice, or chicken stock (page 138)
2 to 3 tablespoons Dijon mustard
1 cup crème fraîche or heavy cream
Salt and pepper
Fresh parsley or chives, chopped

Eat with:
Green salad (page 140)
Tomato & onion salad (page 141)
Watercress

Old-School Cornish Pasties

Makes 4
Ingredients
Short-crust pastry
1¾ cups flour
Good pinch of salt
8 tablespoons cold butter
2 to 3 tablespoons very
   cold water
Beaten egg and milk for
   brushing
Filling
½ pound lean beefsteak
   (rump or stewing)
1 medium onion, finely
   chopped
2 medium potatoes, diced
   small
2 tablespoons stock or oil
Pinch of dried thyme or
   other herb
1 tablespoon finely
   chopped fresh parsley
Salt and freshly ground
   pepper

Eat with:
Homestyle ketchup
   (page 139)
Mash (page 22)
Baked beans
Green-bean spaghetti
   (page 53)

Why Not?
Eat cold in a picnic
lunch.

Traditional potato-and-meat pasties are true food heroes and surprisingly easy to make. Treat the twisty bit on top as a kind of handle. P.S. Originally, half would be filled with jam or fruit so that the tin miners could get a two-in-one meal. Suppose you could try it. . . .

Directions
1. Preheat oven to 400°F.
2. Pastry: Follow the method on page 138.
3. Filling: Cut any fat off the meat and discard. Cut it into chunks. Then into small pieces.
4. Slap it into a bowl with the onion, potato, stock or oil, herbs, salt, and pepper. Mix together.
5. Divide the pastry into 4 pieces. Roll the first piece out into a square on a lightly floured board. Set a 6-inch plate in the middle. Cut around it. Repeat with the remainder for 4 circles. Roll out a bit more if it looks too thick.
6. Heap the filling into the center of each one. Dampen the edges of each circle with a bit of water. Pull the opposite sides up and together over the filling. Join them firmly together, pressing between a thumb and finger.
7. Brush with beaten egg and milk. Set them on a baking sheet.
8. Cook for 15 to 20 minutes, then reduce heat to 375°F for another 20 minutes. Browning fast? Cover with paper.

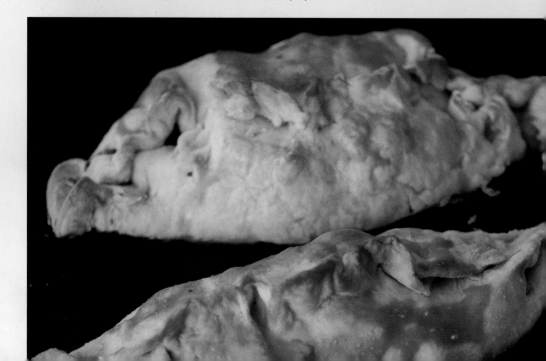

Corned Beef Hash

I love this. It's got style. It's simple—always a good thing. You can chuck it together when you're half asleep, so it makes a great breakfast. The ingredients are pretty basic, so they're always around. The chili twist makes it pretty special.

Directions

1. Bring a pan of lightly salted water to a boil. Add the potato chunks. Boil for 7 to 10 minutes or till just tender. Don't let them crumble. Drain well.
2. Heat the oil in a heavy-bottomed frying pan. Gently fry the onion, garlic, and chili powder for 5 minutes or until softened, not colored.
3. Add the potatoes. Turn with a spatula and cook gently for a few minutes till hot and coated. Put grill on to heat.
4. Break the corned beef up using two forks so that it crumbles into uneven bits. Slap the beef into the mix and turn for a few minutes to heat. Try not to break up the potatoes.
5. Squeeze a good bit of lemon juice into the hash. Stir in the thyme and season with pepper and a little salt. Spoon the mix into a shallow ovenproof dish.
6. Set the dish under the broiler for a few minutes till the top browns. Use this time to poach some eggs, if you like.

Serves 3 to 4
Ingredients
3 medium potatoes, peeled and cut into ½ x 1½-inch chunks
2 tablespoons olive oil
1 large onion, roughly chopped
2 cloves garlic, crushed
Pinch of chili powder
⅓ pound corned beef
½ lemon
A few leaves of fresh thyme
Salt and pepper

Eat with:
Horseradish sauce
Homestyle ketchup (page 139)
A shake of Tabasco
Baked beans
Poached eggs

Why Not?
Substitute any of these for beef:
Cooked ham or bacon
Fried mushrooms
Fried chorizo
Drained tuna

Luscious Shepherd's Pie

Get the best minced lamb or beef from the butcher, or mince your own. Top it off with the creamiest mash baked to crunchy-topped perfection. Liv loves this. (Ain't made from shepherds.)

Directions

1. Heat the olive oil in a large pan. Cook the onion and garlic gently for 5 minutes or till soft, not colored.
2. Chuck in the carrot and celery. Cook to soften for another few minutes.
3. Increase heat and slap in the meat. Turn with a wooden spoon till browned. Too much fat? Spoon it off and chuck it.
4. Add the wine on high heat. Bubble it up to burn off the alcohol.
5. Add the stock or water. Chuck in the tomato purée, Worcestershire sauce, lemon juice, chutney, herbs, salt, and pepper. Stir. Boil for a few minutes.
6. Reduce heat. Cover the pan. Simmer for 30 to 60 minutes. Check and stir occasionally. Add a splash more liquid if it looks dry.
7. Remove. Add the yogurt, if using. Taste and adjust seasoning.
8. Cool for a bit, then top. (If cooking next day, chill ready-topped, or skim the fat off the cold filling and top it with mash. Cook it longer than for same day.)
9. Preheat oven to 400°F.
10. Boil the peeled and quartered spuds in lightly salted water until tender. Drain. Slap back into the pan to sit on the heat, shaking for a few seconds. Add the warm milk, butter, mustard, salt, and pepper. Mash with a masher or fork.
11. Spoon the mash over the meat. Rough up the surface with a fork. Or stick it in a wide-nozzle piping bag and pipe to cover.
12. Bake for 30 to 40 minutes or till crunchy-topped and brown with bubbling edges.

Serves 4
Ingredients
1 tablespoon olive oil
1 onion, diced
3 cloves garlic, crushed
1 carrot, diced
1 stick celery, diced
1 pound minced lamb or ground beef
4 tablespoons red wine
1¼ cups chicken stock (page 138) or water
2 tablespoons tomato purée
Dash of Worcestershire sauce
Squeeze of lemon juice
1 teaspoon mango chutney
Pinch of fresh or dried parsley/thyme/oregano/mint/rosemary
Salt and black pepper
1 to 2 tablespoons plain yogurt (optional)
Topping
2 pounds potatoes
Milk, warmed
Butter
Mustard (optional)
Salt and pepper

Eat with:
Carrot pasta (page 73)
Broccoli (page 72)
Green-bean spaghetti (page 53)

Variations
CHEESY SHEPHERD
At STEP 11, sprinkle with grated Cheddar or Gruyère cheese.
BEAN FREAKS
At STEP 5, add a small can of baked beans.

Chic Champ

Serves 4
Ingredients
2 pounds old floury
   potatoes, unpeeled and
   scrubbed (Yukon Gold
   and russet work)
3 cloves garlic
¾ cup milk
4 green onions, finely
   chopped
3 tablespoons finely
   chopped parsley
4 to 8 tablespoons butter
Salt and pepper

Eat with:
Grilled bacon
Good baked sausages
Portobello mushrooms

Variations
COLCANNON
At STEP 7, add
6 tablespoons drained
shredded cooked
cabbage.
ALIGOT
At STEP 7, add
2 handfuls of grated
Gruyère or Cheddar.

If you've got style and you're a mash fan, then you'll love these traditional Irish mashed potatoes. A bit like designer food, they have so much taste. Not one to eat before going to the gym, I think.

Directions
1. Bring a large pan of lightly salted water to boil. Add the whole potatoes and garlic.
2. Boil for 20 minutes or till tender. Test by poking with a knife.
3. While the spuds cook, heat the milk in a pan with the green onions and parsley for 4 minutes. Set aside.
4. Drain the spuds. Remove and save the garlic. Return the spuds to the pan. Shake over the heat for 2 minutes to dry.
5. Peel the potatoes carefully while still hot. Protect your hands with a tea towel.
6. Tip the spuds back into the cooking pan with two thirds of the butter and the peeled garlic. Mash well till smooth with a masher or fork.
7. Reheat the onion/herb milk till nearly boiling. Use a wooden spoon to beat it into the mash a bit at a time for a creamy, smooth mix. You may not need it all. Taste and season well with salt and pepper. Adjust if you need to.
8. Pile champ on a plate. Slap butter in a hollow in the center. Lovely.

Patatas Bravas

A plate of these big chunks of lovely spuds with a fiery tomato sauce and cooling garlic mayo (aioli) on the side makes a great Spanish-style meal with potatoes.

Directions

1. Sauce: Heat the olive oil in a saucepan. Gently fry the onion till softened but not colored. Add the garlic, chili peppers, and paprika. Cook for another minute.

2. Add the canned or fresh tomatoes, sugar, salt, optional bay leaf, and a few shakes of Tabasco. Bring to a boil, then reduce heat and simmer gently for at least 30 minutes.

3. Patatas: Meanwhile, heat the olive oil for the potatoes in a large pan. Slip the raw or parboiled spuds in (parboiled can be fluffier). Cook over low heat, turning frequently so that they brown evenly for at least 20 minutes. Don't rush the frying. Texture matters.

4. Remove the spuds from the pan when crisp and golden. Quickly fry the whole chili pepper, if using.

5. Strain the sauce, then pour it over and around the potatoes. Sprinkle bits of cilantro over it. Set chili pepper on top. Slap a dollop of aioli on the side. Eat hot or warm. Cool and spicy. Good with chicken or tuna.

Serves 4
Ingredients
Sauce
2 tablespoons olive oil
1 onion, finely chopped
1 clove garlic, crushed
1 to 2 red chillies, de-seeded and finely chopped
½ teaspoon paprika or smoked paprika
14½-ounce can diced tomatoes or 4 large fresh tomatoes, diced
½ teaspoon sugar
Pinch of sea salt
1 bay leaf (optional)
Tabasco sauce
Patatas
3 tablespoons olive oil
1 pound potatoes, peeled and roughly chopped, raw or parboiled for 5 minutes
1 whole chili pepper for topping (optional)
Finely chopped fresh cilantro to garnish
Aioli (page 139)

Eat with:

Tapas (cold meats, hot chorizo, cheeses, shrimp, bread, mussels, olives)

Blinis with Salmon & Lemon Dressing

Serves 4
Ingredients
Salmon
1½ tablespoons sea salt
1½ tablespoons sugar
Finely grated rind of 1
  lemon
1 teaspoon pepper
2 tablespoons finely
  chopped fresh dill
1-pound piece salmon filet
Lemon Dressing
3 tablespoons sugar
¼ cup water
Juice of 2 fat lemons
6 cardamon pods, crushed
⅔ cup olive oil
Salt and pepper
Blinis
1 pound potatoes, peeled
  and quartered
½ cup flour
1 teaspoon baking powder
Pinch of salt
3 medium eggs, beaten
⅔ cup milk
⅔ cup heavy cream
2 egg whites
Sunflower oil and butter

Eat with:
Green leaves
Sour cream
Horseradish sauce
Mustard & dill mayo
  (page 139)

How cool does this look? Curing your own salmon is easy and a perfect excuse to make up these top pancakes. A sharp-tasting mayo and gorgeous lemon salad dressing make this dish plate-heaven.

Directions

1. Salmon: Mix the salt, sugar, lemon rind, pepper, and dill in a bowl.
2. Check the salmon for stray bones. Pull out (use tweezers, if necessary).
3. Lay the fish skin-side down on a bit of plastic wrap that's big enough to wrap it up in. Spread the salt mix evenly over the salmon.
4. Wrap completely in plastic wrap. Set the fish on a large dish or tray. Slap a chopping board on top and then weights or cans to compress it even further.
5. Leave in the fridge for 2 to 3 days to cure. It will seep. Doesn't matter. Ready to eat? Wipe off the cure. Slice thinly with a sharp knife.
6. Lemon dressing: Tip the sugar, water, lemon juice, and cardamon pods in a small pan. Boil. Reduce heat to low. Simmer for 5 minutes. Leave to cool.
7. Whisk in the olive oil and season with salt and pepper.
8. Blinis: Boil the spuds for 10 to 15 minutes or till soft (poke with a knife). Drain. Mash with a masher or fork till really smooth. Cover when cold and place in fridge.
9. Later on or the next day, let the mash return to room temperature. Sift the flour, baking powder, and salt into it. Add the eggs a bit at a time, using a wooden spoon and/or balloon whisk to make a thick, smooth batter. This may require some effort!
10. Heat the milk and cream in a small pan till hot (don't boil). Beat or whisk very slowly into the batter.
11. Whisk the egg whites till soft and fluffy. Fold into the batter with a metal spoon. Don't fuss about the odd bit of white.
12. Heat a bit of oil and butter in a large pan. When this is hot, drop large tablespoons of the mix to cook for 1 to 2 minutes on each side till browning and cooked through.
13. Cover and keep warm till all done.
14. Plate the salmon, blinis, and mayo. Toss leaves in the lemon dressing. Serve. Delicious.

Chocolate

I love a bit of chocolate: licking out the bowl after Mom makes chocolate cake... the smell of the lovely stuff melting down, ready for use in whatever you like. So I stole this chapter for myself, and I'm here to share an awesome ingredient. Hey, it got me into my big passion—cooking. Rules first: chocolate can be difficult (it's a bit like my cat), so treat it with respect. If you're melting it down, do it in a bowl over a pan of lightly simmering water. Don't get water in the bowl or let the bowl touch the water in the pan. The chocolate will seize up and be impossible to deal with. Use the best-quality chocolate (70 percent solids) for top results. Don't keep choc-coated stuff in the fridge—chilling takes the sheen off it. Chocolate's a great mood food. It

sweetens you up. But—don't eat too much. Exercise your cooking skills on my brilliant fruit sundaes, excellent truffle bars, top birthday cake, chocolate fudge pudding, or posh profiteroles. Cocoa's good (very good). Slap it into meringues for a dusky crunch, or get it into crêpes. Short on time? Melt some chocolate down to pour over ice cream or to coat fresh fruit, as in my wacky banana sticks. Get creative. I sculpted my face in it for an art exam—then ate it. I've never had a mate who doesn't love chocolate.

Top Chocolate Soufflé

Serves 4
Ingredients
Melted butter for greasing
3 large egg yolks
2 ounces good dark
   chocolate
⅔ cup milk
¼ cup sugar
6 drops vanilla extract
1 tablespoon cornstarch
2 tablespoons heavy cream
4 large egg whites
Confectioners' sugar for
   dusting (optional)

This one's a high-class bit of chocolate cooking. It's perfect for a posh dinner, to impress someone, or both. Soufflé's got a reputation for being tricky, but this one ain't that hard. It's light and chocolatey—pretty darn special.

Directions

1. Preheat oven to 325°F. Slap a flat baking sheet in there.
2. Using a pastry brush and upward strokes, lightly grease a 6-inch soufflé dish with the melted butter.
3. Separate the eggs into two bowls (with grease-free hands).
4. Break the chocolate up into a small pan with half the milk.
5. Heat extremely gently, stirring a bit with a wooden spoon until smooth. Remove.
6. Mix the egg yolks, sugar, and vanilla in a large bowl. Beat with a whisk till light and moussey.
7. Stir the remaining milk and the cornstarch together till smooth.
8. Add to the egg-yolk mix with the melted chocolate. Stir till smooth.
9. Tip the sauce into a heavy-bottomed pan over gentle heat. Stir constantly and patiently to keep it smooth as it thickens. Remove as it just starts to bubble.
10. Stir in the cream. Return to low heat, stirring for 2 minutes. Scrape the mix into a large bowl.
11. Whisk the egg whites till stiff and voluminous. Tip into the chocolate mix. Fold in with a large metal spoon and big scooping movements.
12. Pour into a prepared soufflé dish. Cook on the baking sheet for 30 minutes till risen, firm on top, but a bit wobbly. If the top browns up early, cover it with parchment paper. (Shut oven door slowly, or the soufflé will sink.) Dust with confectioners' sugar, if you like. Gobble down immediately.

Chocolate Cherry Crêpes

Another variation on the classic. This one is gorgeous. A top contender for Valentine's Day. It's pretty rich, so don't overdo it. Take the ice cream out of the freezer before you get cooking.

Directions

1. Butterscotch sauce: Melt the butter, syrup, and sugar together in a small pan. Boil. Stir in the cream. Reheat gently. Remove.

2. Crêpes: Sift the flour and cocoa into large bowl. Make a dent and crack the egg and add a bit of milk in. Using a balloon whisk or wooden spoon, beat together, adding the milk and water gradually for a smooth batter.

3. Put a crêpe pan or frying pan on high heat. Brush with butter or drop a bit in to melt. Tip to coat the bottom so that your crêpe won't stick when you cook it. (If one does, just chuck it!)

4. Pour 2 to 3 tablespoons of batter into the pan with a swirling motion, twisting to coat. Cook for 1 to 2 minutes.

5. Toss the crêpe to cook the other side or turn neatly with a spatula.

6. Fill: Lay on a plate. Spoon the ice cream, a bit of warm jam or cherries, and a squeeze of lime juice onto one quarter. Fold. Fold again. Drizzle with the butterscotch sauce and lime juice. Dust with confectioners' sugar.

Variations

Try one of these filllings:
CHESTNUT-LIME MAPLE SYRUP
Chopped marrons glacés (candied chestnuts), vanilla ice cream, maple syrup, and lime
BANANA-BUTTERSCOTCH
Sliced banana, vanilla ice cream, butterscotch sauce, and lemon
PEACH-RASPBERRY
Sliced peach or nectarine, vanilla ice cream, and fresh raspberry sauce
MANGO-LIME-COCONUT
Sliced mango, coconut ice cream, maple syrup, and lime

Chocolate Nut Brownies

Makes 16 brownies
Ingredients
2 ounces dark chocolate
8 tablespoons soft butter
1½ cups brown sugar
2 eggs, beaten
½ cup flour
Pinch of salt
½ teaspoon baking powder
2 cups walnuts or pecans
6 drops vanilla extract
Grated rind of ½ large
  orange

Don't panic. They'll crack up in the pan. But it's a cool look, and these chewy brownies taste fantastic. Make a batch on the weekend to snack on through the week. Take them in to school to share with mates. Throw some raisins in for a fruity twist. Don't like nuts? Go for my truffle bars.

Directions
1. Preheat oven to 375°F.
2. Grease and line the bottom of an 8-inch square, shallow baking pan.
3. Put a pan of water on to heat until it simmers.
4. Break the chocolate into a heatproof bowl. Set the bowl on the pan. Check that the base of the bowl sits clear of the gently simmering water.
5. When the chocolate melts, stir till smooth with a wooden spoon. Take it off the heat.
6. Tip the butter and sugar into a large bowl. Beat hard with a wooden spoon till it's soft and creamy.
7. Dribble the beaten eggs into the butter mix gradually, beating furiously as you go. Stir in the melted chocolate, flour, salt, baking powder, nuts, vanilla, and orange rind. Transfer to the pan and level gently.
8. Bake for 35 to 40 minutes. Test with a toothpick. It should come out clean. Leave in the pan for 15 minutes.
9. Divide into 16 squares with a sharp knife. Remove with a spatula. Set on a cooling rack.

Excellent Chocolate Truffle Bars

Like brownies, but better, I think. These are nut-free, smooth, and deeply chocolatey. They're perfect with a cup of tea or at the end of a meal with a pot of coffee. Why not decorate them to look like posh chocolates? Sure to be a hit whenever.

Directions

1. Preheat oven to 350°F. Line an 8-inch square baking pan with parchment paper.
2. Break the chocolate up. Tip it and the butter into a heatproof bowl.
3. Set it over a pan of gently simmering water, checking that the base of the bowl doesn't touch the water. Stir together as they melt.
4. Take the bowl off the heat. Beat in the sugar and vanilla.
5. Use a balloon whisk to beat in the eggs. Sift in the flour and salt. Give the mix a good beating.
6. Tip the truffle into the pan. Cook for 35 minutes. Check for doneness with a toothpick. You want it still a bit moist.
7. Remove from oven to cool on a rack. Cut into bar shapes after 10 minutes. Use a spatula to remove from the pan when cold. Make icing and decorate!

Makes 8 bars
Ingredients
7 ounces dark chocolate
10 tablespoons butter
1¼ cups sugar
2 teaspoons vanilla extract
2 large eggs
1 extra yolk
⅔ cup flour
Pinch of salt

Icing
Stir a few drops of water into 6 tablespoons sifted confectioners' sugar for a stiffish mix. Pipe decorations.

Frozen Chocolate Banana Sticks

Makes 8 to 12
Ingredients
4 bananas
8 to 12 Popsicle sticks or
    wooden skewers
10 ounces good chocolate
    (dark or milk)

Variations
CRISPY
Mix crisp rice cereal
into part or all of the
chocolate.
COCONUT
Sprinkle shredded
coconut over the
chocolate.

Why Not?
**Bake chocolate
bananas.** Preheat
oven to 400°F. Make a
slit down unpeeled
bananas. Slip some
chocolate buttons or
bits of chocolate inside.
Wrap in foil. Cook for
10 to 15 minutes.

Make apple sticks.
Dip apples on sticks
into melted chocolate.
Set upside down on
a nonstick surface
to dry.

Dip fruit on stalks in
chocolate. (Try
cherries, strawberries,
kiwifruit).

Now, these look a bit weird. They could almost pass for pieces of art. Think banana split without the ice cream. They make a tasty laugh at the end of a meal. Make up a load to cool down a party.

Directions

1. Lay a sheet of wax paper on a baking sheet.
2. Peel the bananas.
3. Cut each in half or diagonally into 4 pieces. Shove a Popsicle stick or skewer into each cut end to make a lollipop.
4. Lay the lollies on the paper. Slap into the freezer for an hour or till completely frozen.
5. Bring a small pan of water to simmer gently. Set a bowl over the top, checking that it's clear of the water.
6. Break up the chocolate. Slap into the bowl. Once it melts, stir to a smooth sauce.
7. Fetch the bananas. Dunk into the chocolate to coat, or use a spoon.
8. Lay back on the baking sheet. Freeze. Store in freezer bags or boxes.

Sleepover Breakfast Brioche

There's nothing like tearing into one of these in the morning. But be warned—I've burned myself on the oozy chocolate inside many a time. Let it cool for a second or two before you dig in. These look, smell, and taste so good, you can't help thinking they should be for sale.

Makes 12
Ingredients
2¼ cups bread flour
1 packet (0.25 ounce) active
   dry yeast
Pinch of fine salt
3 medium eggs, beaten
3½ tablespoons sugar
¼ cup warm milk
8 tablespoons soft butter
12 squares from a bar of
   dark chocolate or a good
   Belgian chocolate spread
Extra beaten egg for
   brushing

Variations
OTHER FILLINGS
Apricot or strawberry
   jam
Chocolate-hazelnut
   spread
No filling (for plain)

Directions

1. By mixer: Tip the flour, yeast, salt, eggs, sugar, and milk into a mixer bowl with a dough hook. Beat for 5 minutes. **By hand:** Sift the flour and salt into a large bowl, then add the sugar and yeast. Tip the eggs and milk into a dent in the center. Beat to a smooth dough with hands or a wooden spoon. Set the dough on a floured board. Knead, punch, slap, and stretch for 5 minutes for a smooth, elastic ball.

2. Now, smear a bit of the butter onto the dough. Push, punch, and squeeze it right in till amalgamated. Repeat till all the butter's used, the dough shiny and bubbly.

3. Put the dough into a large bowl. Cover with plastic wrap. Chill in fridge for at least 1 hour or overnight if cooking for breakfast.

4. Grease individual brioche pans and set on a baking sheet, or grease a muffin pan.

5. Knead the dough. Divide into 12 smooth, flat circles. Set a chocolate square or half a teaspoon of chocolate spread in the center. Draw the dough up around it. Join with firm pressure and a bit of beaten egg for a smooth ball and no leakage.

6. Drop into the pans join-side down. Leave in a warm place to double in size. Preheat oven to 400°F.

7. Brush with the beaten egg. Bake 12 to 15 minutes till browned and high. Cool on a rack for 3 minutes or eat cold.

Hot Chocolate-Fudge Pudding

Serves 4
Ingredients
1 teaspoon instant coffee
1½ tablespoon boiling water
8 tablespoons soft butter
½ cup sugar
2 medium eggs
1 teaspoon vanilla extract
¾ cup flour
1¼ teaspoons baking powder
Pinch of salt
¼ cup cocoa powder
Confectioners' sugar for
   topping

Sauce
⅔ cup hot water
¾ cup brown sugar
1 tablespoon cocoa

You've got to trust me on this one. When you get it in the dish, it looks like a cruel joke. Get it out of the oven, though, and you've got this delicious chocolate sponge over a delectable sauce.

Directions

1. Preheat oven to 350°F.
2. Grease the bottom and sides of a 1-quart ovenproof dish.
3. Mix the coffee and boiling water, stirring to dissolve.
4. Slap the butter and sugar into a large bowl. Beat with a wooden spoon till light, pale, and creamy.
5. Beat the eggs with a fork. Add to the mix bit by bit, beating as you go. Add a pinch of flour if it threatens to curdle. When creamy, add the vanilla. Sift the flour, baking powder, salt, and cocoa in. Add the liquid coffee.
6. Fold everything together using a large metal spoon and light scooping movements till it just falls off the end of the spoon.
7. Spoon into the dish.
8. **Sauce:** Put the water on to boil. Mix the brown sugar and cocoa in a bowl. Stir in the hot water. Pour over the sponge batter. Looks crazy. Stay with it!
9. Set the dish in a roasting pan with enough boiling water to reach halfway up the sides. Cook for 45 minutes or longer till risen. A toothpick should come out clean. Dust with confectioners' sugar. Eat hot, warm, or cold and/or with ice cream (page 117).

Chocolate Fruit Sundaes

Make it simple or extravagant. Chuck loads of fruit in there. Not just for Sundays.

Directions

1. Ice cream: Tip the egg yolks into a bowl. Beat well with a fork.

2. Pour the milk into a pan. Add the sugar and vanilla. Heat gently, stirring with a wooden spoon to dissolve the sugar. Whack the heat up. Bring the milk just to the boiling point (bubbling). Remove.

3. Tip it into the egg, stirring continuously. Tip back into the pan.

4. Heat gently, stirring till the custard thickens enough to coat the back of the spoon. (If it curdles at any stage, remove and beat till smooth.)

5. Cool the custard, then beat the yogurt in with a balloon whisk. Churn in an ice-cream maker or pour the cream into a bowl or freezer bag. Freeze till it starts to solidify. Remove and re-whisk. Return to freezer. Remove 10 minutes before you need it.

6. Wash and prepare your chosen fruit.

7. Chocolate sauce: Break the chocolate into a heatproof bowl. Place the bowl over a pan of gently simmering water. Add the butter, syrup, and water. Melt, then stir till smooth. Remove from heat. Add the vanilla extract.

8. Chuck alternate layers of ice cream, fruit, optional meringue, and chocolate sauce into glasses.

Serves 4

Ingredients

Good store-bought vanilla ice cream or make your own:

6 egg yolks
⅔ cup milk
⅓ cup sugar
Seeds of 1 vanilla pod, or ½ to 1 teaspoon vanilla bean paste
1 cup plain yogurt

Choice of fresh fruit

Pitted, chopped or peeled
Cherries
Raspberries
Strawberries
Pears
Bananas
Blackberries

My chocolate sauce

4 ounces dark chocolate
1 tablespoon butter
2 tablespoons golden syrup, or 1½ tablespoons corn syrup and ½ tablespoon molasses or honey
2 tablespoons water
1 tablespoon vanilla extract

Meringue

3 to 4 plain or chocolate meringues (page 121), crumbled

Why Not?

Make Knickerbocker Glory. Stack loads more fresh fruit layered with chopped gelatin (page 126), fresh raspberry syrup (page 133), and crumbled almond macaroons.

Best Chocolate Cake

Serves 10
Ingredients
½ cup flour
⅔ cup ground almonds
8 ounces good-quality dark
  chocolate (at least 70
  percent cocoa)
4 tablespoons butter
¼ cup brown sugar
6 eggs, separated
A little grated orange rind
  (optional)
1 cup sugar
Confectioners' sugar for
  dusting

Makes a fine teatime or birthday-style treat. The dip in the middle's deliberate. Love it.

Directions

1. Preheat oven to 350°F.
2. Grease and line the bottom and sides of an 8-inch loose-based or clip-sided baking pan with parchment paper.
3. Sift the flour and almonds into a big bowl.
4. Put the chocolate squares and butter into a heatproof bowl. Set over a pan of gently simmering water. Melt. Stir till smooth. Remove. Cool a bit.
5. Whisk the brown sugar and egg yolks together for a few minutes to get a pale, frothy mousse. Add the flour mix, chocolate, and rind, if using. Fold lightly to mix using a large metal spoon and scooping movements.
6. Whisk the egg whites till soft and fluffy. Add the sugar gradually for a stiff meringue. Fold gently into the cake mix. Tip into the pan. Bake for 45 to 50 minutes till crisp on top, squishy inside. Test with a toothpick—should exit a bit sticky.
7. Cool on rack. The cake will sink, but that's OK. Peel the paper off with care when cold. Dust with confectioners' sugar.

Posh Chocolate Profiteroles

Retro French classic. Crisp pastry puffs meet soft vanilla cream and rich chocolate drizzle. Stack 'em up for posh puddings, teatimes, dinner parties, parties. Gorgeous.

Directions

1. **Puffs:** Sift the flour, salt, and sugar onto a large piece of parchment paper.
2. Tip the water and butter into a medium-size pan. Melt gently. Increase the heat to bring to a boil. Immediately slide the dry ingredients off the paper into the boiling liquid. Beat like mad with a wooden spoon till the dough makes a ball. Whip off the heat. Beat furiously for a few minutes to make a smooth paste. Tip the paste onto the parchment paper. Leave for at least 10 minutes.
3. Preheat oven to 400°F. Grease two large baking sheets.
4. Slap the paste into a bowl. Beat the egg in a little at a time. You may not need all the egg, or you may need more of it. The final mix needs to be soft and glossy and should just drop off your spoon.

5. Heap teaspoons of mix spaced apart on the baking sheets. Gently flatten any spikes with your fingers. Sprinkle a few drops of cold water on the trays between puffs to aid rising.
6. Cook for 20 to 25 minutes or till browned and crisp. Pierce the base of each with a skewer. Cook for 5 minutes upside down to crisp. Cool on a rack.
7. **Filling:** Whisk the cream till just stiff. Fold in the sugar and vanilla. Spoon into a piping bag with a large nozzle or a plastic bag with a hole cut in the corner. Pipe through the hole to fill the puffs.
8. Set the puffs on plates or bowls. Drizzle 'em with chocolate sauce.

Makes 20 to 25
Ingredients
Puffs
1 cup flour
Pinch of salt
Pinch of sugar
1 cup water
6 tablespoons butter
2 large eggs, beaten
Filling
2½ cups heavy cream
1 to 2 tablespoons
    confectioners' sugar, sifted
A few drops vanilla extract
Sauce
Hot chocolate sauce
    (page 117)

Variations

COFFEE ÉCLAIRS
At STEP 5, pipe éclair-style lengths of dough well apart on the baking sheets. At STEP 7, pipe cream into each éclair. At STEP 8, make up a batch of **coffee icing:** Beat 2¼ cups sifted confectioners' sugar with 2 tablespoons of very strong, hot coffee with a wooden spoon till soft and just runny. Dip the top of each éclair into the icing. Let them set.

ICE-CREAM BUNS
Make ice-cream buns. Fill large puffs with ice cream (page 117). Drizzle with chocolate sauce. Eat at once.

Chocolate Mayo Cake with Fudge Frosting

Serves 10
Ingredients
2 cups flour
1 teaspoon baking powder
1 teaspoon baking soda
1 cup sugar
1 cup mayonnaise
¼ cup cocoa powder
1 cup boiling water
1 teaspoon vanilla extract
Extra butter or oil for
   greasing

Fudge frosting
2 ⅓ cup confectioners'
   sugar
⅓ cup cocoa powder
8 tablespoons butter
3 to 4 tablespoons water

Run out of eggs or just fancy an amazing cake? It's all chocolate. You won't taste the mayo bit. P.S. The fudge icing's special.

Directions

1. Preheat oven to 350°F. Grease an 8-inch round cake pan.
2. Sift the flour, baking powder, baking soda, and sugar into a bowl. Beat in the mayo with a wooden spoon. It'll look lumpy, but don't worry.
3. Pour boiling water over the cocoa and vanilla in a heatproof bowl. Stir to dissolve.
4. Beat this liquid into the flour mix until it's soft and creamy.
5. Pour the batter into the cake pan. Bake 40 minutes or till cake starts to shrink from the edges. You can also check that a toothpick comes out clean—then it's done. Cool in the pan for 10 minutes, then transfer to a rack. Make sure it's completely cool before frosting.
6. Frosting: Sift the sugar and cocoa into a bowl. Melt the butter and water together without boiling. Beat gradually into the sugar mix till smooth but not too runny— you may not need to use all of the liquid to get the consistency right. Pour over the cake, letting it drip over the sides, or spread it neatly around.

Why Not?
Make icing (page 113) and decorate!

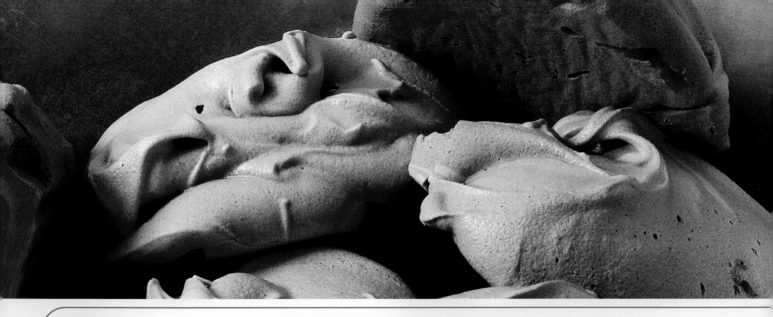

Cocoa-Crunch Meringues

I love meringues, but these chocolatey ones just blow me away. Stack them on a plate with some plain white ones for stunning looks and dramatic contrast.

Directions

1. Preheat oven to 250°F.
2. Line 2 large baking sheets with parchment paper.
3. Stick your egg whites in a very clean bowl—I use a copper one. Whisk with an electric or hand whisk till you get soft, white peaks. Add the sugar a bit at a time, whisking as you go till the meringue is really stiff and white.
4. Sift the cocoa over the mix. Fold it in using a large metal spoon and big scooping movements—the odd whitish streak is fine.
5. Get the mix onto the baking sheets using two large spoons. Make a lot of small meringues or a few big ones. Use one spoon to push the mix off the other. Leave a bit of space between meringues to allow spreading. If you

want to get fancy, use a piping bag with a medium-to-large nozzle.
6. Stick the baking sheets in your oven. Bake for 1½ hours. Turn off the heat.
7. Leave the meringues there till quite cold. Peel them carefully, off the paper. Store in an airtight container for up to 2 months.

Makes 8
Ingredients
4 egg whites
1¼ cups sugar
1 tablespoon cocoa powder

Eat with:
Macerated strawberries (slice large berries, sprinkle with a bit of confectioners' sugar and lemon juice, and chill till needed), sliced peaches, or mangoes marinated in lime syrup (page 137)

Variation
PAVLOVA
Spread the mix into two flat circles on the baking sheets. Cook for the same time as individual meringues. When cold, sandwich with whipped cream and fresh berries.

Sweet Stuff

Everyone loves sweets, and Verity is no exception. We're talking elite eating here. Quality cooking. OK, there's sugar playing in most of these beautiful dishes, but no problem. Just don't inhale the lot yourself while chained to the sofa. Balance a slice of something yummy with a game or two. Making this gorgeous stuff's like culinary-style exercise anyway. You get a workout in perfecting key techniques like whisking, beating, grating, folding in, and creaming. Dessert is also a great excuse to eat fruit. Baked apples with dates (meringue-topped or not). Cinnamon toast with summer plums. Whole-orange cake (yup, you use the whole fruit—except the seeds). Lemon gelatin. Summer pudding. Raspberry ripple fool. Stylish frozen treats majoring in fruitiness. All these dishes are perfect for serving when you've got mates over. For special dinners. Birthdays. Weekends when you're relaxing. For treating a parent who's been behaving. (Or maybe you need a treat.) Game, set, and match.

Perfect Pancakes

Serves 4
Ingredients
2 eggs separated at room temperature
2/3 cup milk
4 tablespoons melted butter
1 cup flour
3½ teaspoons sugar
2 pinches salt
2 teaspoons baking powder
Extra melted butter for brushing

Cooking for breakfast?
Great with maple syrup, blackberries (or any berries), and crisp bacon.

Eating for lunch?
Try with chopped smoked salmon and sour cream.

Teatime?
Good with jam (page 139), cream, and strawberries, or just butter.

I fell in love with these while visiting America. They're light and fluffy with a golden finish and are easily adapted for any eating situation. OK, they take a minute more to make than crêpes, but so what? Stack and style any way you want. Sweet or savory, we're talking quality.

Directions
1. Beat the egg yolks well with a fork. Add the milk and melted butter till blended.
2. Sift the flour, sugar, salt, and baking powder into a large third bowl. Add the egg/milk mix to it. Stir in gradually and gently for a lump-free batter.
3. Whisk the egg whites until they are stiff and white but still soft, not overbeaten.
4. Tip the whites into the batter, then fold in as gently as you can using a large metal spoon and soft scooping movements.
5. Heat a heavy-bottomed frying pan. Coat with a bit of melted butter (a pastry brush works). Drop tablespoons of the mix in when hot enough.
6. Cook 1 to 2 minutes per side. Should be golden on the outside with puffed-up middles.
7. Eat now or keep warm.

Sweet Shortcakes

Like scones, but double-stacked, with a sweeter, crumbly texture. Butter and jam them up, or get some cream and fresh fruit in there. Perfect with a cup of tea—preferably from a proper teapot.

Directions

1. Preheat oven to 450°F.
2. Sift the flour, baking powder, and salt into a large bowl.
3. Chuck the butter in, cutting into small bits. Get it into the flour by rubbing the two between your fingertips, hand held over the bowl, till the mix looks like breadcrumbs.
4. Slap in the sugar and cream. Mix with a fork. Pull the mix into a soft ball with your fingers. Handle lightly now.
5. Set the dough on a lightly floured board. Shape and smooth lightly before gently rolling out till ½ inch thick.
6. Cut into 2-inch rounds with a cookie cutter. Don't twist the dough.
7. Reform remaining dough gently. Re-roll and cut again.
8. Set half the cakes spaced apart on a greased baking sheet.
9. Brush lightly with the melted butter. Set another circle firmly on top of each cake to double the stack.
10. Bake for 10 to 15 minutes till golden and cooked through. Cool on a rack.

Serves 6
Ingredients
2¼ cups flour
3 teaspoons baking powder
Pinch of salt
10 tablespoons soft butter
⅓ cup sugar
⅔ cup heavy cream
2 tablespoons melted butter

Eat with:
Strawberries (or any other fruit)
Fresh whipped cream
Jam

Lemon Dessert

Serves 4
Ingredients
2 large lemons
2 cups cold water
½ cup sugar
1 packet (0.25-ounce)
  gelatin

Variations
FLAT GELATIN
Don't whisk it.
ST. CLEMENT'S
Use 1 lemon and
1 small orange.
ORANGE
Use 2 oranges or
blood oranges, or 4
clementines instead of
lemons.
VEGETARIAN
Substitute gelatin with
agar.

Feeling ill?
Ask someone to
make it for you!

You'll impress your mates with this one. Homemade gelatin's so much tastier and healthier than the rubbish packaged stuff. This one's got the sharpest taste and neatest look. Get yourself some interesting molds to pour it into.

Directions
1. Pare the rind thinly from the lemons with a sharp knife or peeler. Rough strips are fine. Avoid the bitter white pith.
2. In a large bowl, soak the gelatin in half the cold water to soften.
3. Meanwhile, slap the rind, sugar, and the rest of the water into a pan. Bring to a boil for 1 minute. Reduce heat. Simmer very gently with the lid on for 15 minutes.
4. Immediately add to the gelatin, stirring until dissolved.
5. Squeeze the lemon juice into the syrup through a strainer.
6. Refrigerate. When it looks like it's setting, whisk it hard to create white bubbles.
7. Pour into glasses or splash a gelatin mold or glass dish with a bit of water. Pour the gelatin in. Refrigerate. When it's set, get your spoon in there.

Whole-Orange Cake

This wacky mix transforms itself into the lightest, loveliest citrusy cake. Make it for afternoon tea or for parties.

Directions

1. Stick the oranges in a medium pan. Cover with water.
2. Boil, then reduce heat. Simmer for 2 to 3 hours with a lid on. Add more water when needed. Remove the fruit. Leave to cool.
3. Slice the fruit in two. Get the seeds out and chuck them.
4. Stick the whole fruit in a processor or blender. Blitz till smooth.
5. Preheat oven to 350°F.
6. Grease and line a 9-inch clip-sided pan with parchment paper.
7. Crack the eggs into a large bowl with the sugar. Whisk to a pale, thick mousse till doubled in volume using an electric or hand whisk.
8. Tip the orange blitz, baking powder, and almonds into the mousse. Fold together with a large metal spoon using a few big scooping movements. Handle gently to keep the air in.
9. Pour into the pan. Bake for 50 to 60 minutes. Insert a toothpick to test doneness. It should come out clean. Cool in the pan.
10. Release the pan. Peel the paper away. Sift confectioners' sugar over, and serve with fresh raspberries, if desired.

Serves 4 to 6
Ingredients
2 large unwaxed oranges
6 medium eggs
1¼ cups sugar
1 teaspoon baking powder
2⅓ cup ground almonds
Fresh raspberries (optional)
Confectioners' sugar (optional)

Eat with:
Citrus cream
Mix mascarpone, confectioners' sugar, lemon rind, and orange and lemon juice into a smooth cream.

Variations
OTHER ORANGE OPTIONS
Try substituting 2 large blood oranges or 4 to 6 clementines for regular oranges.

Classic Crème Caramel

Serves 4
Ingredients
Butter for greasing
2 tablespoons cold water
⅓ cup sugar
2 teaspoons boiling water
3 large eggs
1 cup milk
2 tablespoons sugar
½ teaspoon vanilla extract

Enjoy the light, silky texture of the baked custard sitting in its soft, golden caramel sauce. This classic is comfort-food chic. Make it to cheer yourself up. Dress it up with fruit and cream for something special.

Directions

1. Preheat oven to 325°F.
2. Grease a 1-pint dish with butter.
3. Tip the cold water and sugar into a small pan over low heat. Stir to dissolve with a wooden spoon. Increase heat. Stop stirring to allow the syrup to caramelize. Boil till it turns a deep golden brown. Don't let it burn.
4. Carefully remove the pan from heat and add the boiling water. Pour the liquid into the buttered dish, tilting it to swirl the toffee over the bottom and a bit up the sides. Set aside.
5. Beat the eggs and milk together with a balloon whisk, adding the sugar and vanilla. Set a strainer over the caramelized baking dish. Pour the egg mix through it.

6. Set the dish in a roasting pan. Pour cold water into the pan to reach halfway up the sides of the dish.
7. Cook for 45 to 50 minutes till just set. It keeps cooking, so you want it to have a bit of wobble.
8. Take it out of the pan to cool. Chill.
9. To turn out: Set a plate over the dish. Invert. Give it a shake. If it doesn't loosen, turn it back. Run a thin knife around the custard with care. Try again.

Baked Apple Meringues

Mix and match these bad boys: some with meringue on top, some not. Either way, they're deliciously juicy and full of awesomeness. A really great one to cheer up autumn days going into winter.

Directions

1. Preheat oven to 350°F. Grease an ovenproof dish large enough for all the apples (use double ingredients for big family dinners).
2. Use a sharp knife to cut a continuous line around the circumference of each fruit to stop them from bursting. Set them in the dish.
3. Tip the chopped dates into a small bowl. Mix with the orange rind and juice. Stuff the mix into the center of the cored fruit.
4. Mix the brown sugar and spice. Sprinkle this mix on top of each apple, then dot the lot with dabs of butter.
5. Pour the juice or sherry into the dish. Bake till nearly cooked through. This could take 45 minutes or much longer if using larger apples or a harder variety. Keep checking.
6. **Meringue:** Whisk the egg whites till soft, white, and peaky. Whisk half the sugar in, bit by bit, till the mix is very stiff. Stir in the rest.
7. Remove the fruit from the oven. Using a spoon and sharp knife, peel the top bit of skin off 2 apples. Spoon or pipe the meringue on these stripped tops. Return to oven. For soft meringue, bake for 15 minutes. Crisper tops will take longer, but watch that the apples don't collapse.
8. Eat hot or warm. Also great cold with yogurt. Try reheating them.

Makes 4
Ingredients
4 cooking apples, washed and cored
A few fresh or dried dates, chopped
Grated rind and juice of 1 large orange
2 tablespoons brown sugar
1 teaspoon allspice
Butter for topping
½ cup orange juice, apple juice, or sherry

Meringue
2 egg whites
⅓ cup sugar

Variation
Fill the apple cavities with a mix of syrup and butter or with butter, sherry, and crumbled almond cookies.

129

Jam Soufflé Omelette

Serves 1
Ingredients
Filling
1 to 2 tablespoons best jam
   (page 138)
A little water

Omelette
2 large fresh eggs (organic
   if possible)
1 teaspoon sugar
1 tablespoon milk
A little butter
Confectioners' sugar

Seems a little crazy, but you'll be glad you made it. It's heavy on the wow factor (both looks and taste) and light in the mouth. Sweet, puffy omelette meets hot, jammy sauce. I use a 6-inch pan for this. Make your own jam, or buy a good, fruity one.

Directions

1. Preheat broiler to medium.
2. Tip the jam and water into a small pan to melt. Heat gently, stirring with a wooden spoon until sticky and just runny. Put aside until you need it.
3. Separate the eggs. Slap the yolks into one bowl, the whites into another. Put the sugar and milk in with the yolks. Beat them into a moussey froth (may take time). Whisk the whites with a clean whisk so that they stand in soft peaks. Don't overwhisk.
4. Put a frying pan onto gentle heat with a little butter.
5. Tip the whisked whites into the yolk mix. Use a spatula to cut or fold them till just mixed. Keeping air in is vital, so the odd blobs don't matter.
6. When the butter foams, slide the mix in. Cook for 1 to 2 minutes or till just set.

7. Slide the pan under the broiler but not too close to the heat for 2 minutes. The omelette should rise. Remove when just set and just coloring.
8. Slide onto a warm plate (use a spatula to help). Pour the jam over half. Use a spatula to fold the other half over. Sift a little confectioners' sugar over the top. Magnificent enough for a special dinner.

Cinnamon Toast with Summer Plums

Mmm ... the bread toasts to a lovely crisp top while the bottom soaks up the luscious juices from the plums. It's all set off with a buttery cinnamon sweetness. Honestly, you've got to try this.

Directions

1. Preheat oven to 375°F.
2. Cream the butter and cinnamon in a small bowl.
3. Spread two-thirds of the mixture evenly over the bread.
4. Set the bread in a well-buttered shallow ovenproof dish. It may creep up the sides, but that doesn't matter.
5. Fill each plum center with the brown sugar. Place the plums cut-side down evenly over the bread. Dot the remaining butter-cinnamon mix over the top with extra brown sugar.
6. Cover with a bit of buttered parchment paper and bake for 20 minutes.
7. Uncover and cook for 5 minutes or till the bread is crisp and browned.
8. Remove. Sprinkle with a bit of sugar if you like.

Serves 4
Ingredients
6 tablespoons soft butter
1 teaspoon ground cinnamon
4 slices of thick white bread, crustless
8 to 10 large ripe plums (1¼ to 1½ pounds), cut in half and pitted
⅔ cup brown sugar (or cane sugar for extra crunch), plus extra for topping

Summer Pudding

Serves 6
Ingredients
⅔ cup sugar
⅔ cup orange juice
2 tablespoons lemon juice
1 tablespoon crème de cassis
2 pounds mixed soft fruit (e.g., rhubarb, strawberries, blueberries, raspberries)
2 to 3 mint leaves (optional)
6 to 8 thin slices of white bread
Fruit for decorating (optional)
Cream for piping (optional)

Don't be put off by the bread. It soaks up those oozy, fruity juices and transforms itself into something extraordinary. P.S. Cheat in winter. Buy frozen summer fruit.

Directions

1. Tip the sugar, fruit juices, and crème de cassis into a large pan on gentle heat to dissolve the sugar. Bring to a boil, then decrease heat.

2. Add the rhubarb, if using (cook 3 minutes), then the strawberries, blueberries, half the raspberries, any other fruit, and mint, if using. Simmer for 5 minutes or till the fruit softens but still holds its shape. Add the remaining raspberries. Set aside.

3. Cut the crusts off the bread. Use the slices to line a 1½-quart bowl. Put the first slice in the bottom, then cut or tear the rest to line the sides. Don't leave gaps or the fruit will leak. Overlap a bit if you want. Neatness doesn't matter.

4. Spoon the fruit into the lining. Include some juices to soak through and flavor the bread. Save excess juice for later.

5. Seal by covering the top with as much bread as you need. Set a plate on top, followed by weights or a jar to compress. Fridge it.

6. Turn out: Remove the plate and weights. Put a serving plate on top. Holding the plate and bowl tightly together, invert in one swift move. Shake it a bit. If it won't drop out, turn it back up. Run a thin knife around it. Repeat the first maneuver.

7. Spoon any extra juice over the top if there are any bald patches. Add the fresh fruit for decoration, if using. Pipe cream on there if you want to.

Raspberry Ripple Fool

For my money, fresh raspberries are the best summer fruit and work brilliantly in this creamy dessert. It's got a homestyle raspberry sauce plus mashed berries. Stick it in a bowl to eat on the sofa or in a glass to show it off for company. Enjoy with a crunchy cookie.

Serves 3 to 4
Ingredients
- 1 pound (3½ cups) fresh raspberries
- 2 tablespoons sugar or more to taste
- 1 to 2 teaspoons rose water or sugared water
- 1¾ cups heavy or whipping cream

Directions

1. Put half the raspberries into a pan with half the sugar, the rose water, and a splash of water. Simmer very gently until they start to release juice.

2. Set a strainer over a bowl. Push the contents of the pan through with a wooden spoon. Leave the raspberry syrup to cool.

3. Whisk the cream up with the rest of the sugar till soft and pillowy (not too stiff or grainy).

4. Mash the remaining raspberries with a fork. Fold into the cream.

5. Stir the raspberry syrup gently into the cream for a ripple effect, or layer the raspberry cream and syrup in glasses or bowls. Chill.

Variations
SPEEDY FOOL
Whip the cream and sugar. Mash in ripe mango, blackberries, blueberries, strawberries, or lightly poached rhubarb.
CRUNCHY FOOL
Crumble in meringue, almond macaroons, or ginger cookies.

Steamed Winter Pudding

The classic English old-school pudding. Everyone loves it. It's rich and warming. OK, it's a bit of a challenge, but for a lovely soft sponge and hot, sweet syrup, it's worth it. Make custard to go with it!

Directions

1. Fill a steamer ⅓ full of water. Or fill a large saucepan with water to come ⅓ the way up the sides of a 1-quart heatproof dish (or a 5-cup dish for a saucier pudding). Bring to a simmer.

2. Grease the inside of the dish well with extra butter.

3. Spoon the golden syrup (or substitute), juice, and half the rind into a small heavy-bottomed pan. Melt gently and stir to amalgamate.

4. Tip the breadcrumbs into the syrup mix. Pour into the dish.

5. Now, slap the butter and sugar into a large, warm bowl. Use a wooden spoon to beat the two together till pale and light in texture.

6. Tip a little beaten egg into this mix while still beating. Continue bit by bit till it's all in. If the mix starts to separate, add a pinch of flour. If the bowl and ingredients are warm, that shouldn't happen.

7. Sift the flour into the creamed mix. Add the rest of the orange and/or lemon rind. Using a large metal spoon and large scooping movements, fold the dry ingredients into the mix together with 1 tablespoon water. You want the mix to be soft enough to drop off the end of the spoon. Add a bit more water if you need it.

8. Scoop and pour the mix on top of the syrup in the dish. It will look weird, but that's OK.

9. Cut out a piece of foil that will more than cover the top of the dish. Grease one side of the foil, then make a 2-inch fold across the middle so that it can expand when the pudding rises. Place the foil buttered-side down over the top. Fold it down, then tie tightly with string (get someone to help). Trim off most of the excess foil, but leave a fringe around it.

10. Put the dish into your steamer or pan of simmering water. Steam for 1½ hours. Check and top up the water levels every 10 minutes or so.

11. Remove. Cut the string to release and remove the foil. Run a knife between the dish and the pudding to help release it. Place a large plate over the top. Quickly and carefully invert the plate. The boiling syrup sauce will flood out. Shake the bowl gently to release the pudding. Eat with custard.

Serves 4

Ingredients

Butter for greasing
3 tablespoons golden syrup, or 1½ tablespoons corn syrup and ½ tablespoon molasses or honey
Juice of 2 oranges (or 1 orange and 1 lemon)
Rind of 2 oranges (or 1 orange and 1 lemon)
2 tablespoons fresh white breadcrumbs
8 tablespoons soft butter
½ cup sugar
2 eggs, beaten
1 cup flour
1½ teaspoons baking powder
½ teaspoon salt
1 to 2 tablespoons cold water
String for pudding

Custard

¼ cup milk
1 split vanilla pod, a few drops vanilla extract, or a strip of lemon peel
3 egg yolks
3 teaspoons sugar
2 teaspoons cornstarch

Heat the milk in a medium saucepan with the vanilla pod, extract, or lemon peel. Remove when it just boils (don't let it boil over). Take the pod out, if using. Slap the egg yolks in a large bowl with the sugar and cornstarch. Mix well. Tip the hot milk slowly into the mix while stirring with a wooden spoon. Tip back into the pan. Stir over low heat till thickish. Don't boil—it'll curdle. Stir like mad. Place the pan in cold water if it gets grainy. Pour into a jug. Eat hot, cold, or warm.

Four Stylish Frozen Treats

Serves 4
Ingredients
3 to 4 lemons, washed and dried
1½ cups confectioners' sugar
1 cup heavy cream
1 cup plain yogurt
3 tablespoons very cold water

Eat with:
Cakes
Fruit salads
Sundaes

As you get older, good old Mr. Goodbar doesn't quite do it anymore. Really, you want something different and lighter. These four ices are so easy and don't require any fancy equipment. Perfect for summer. Brilliant for parties.

Tangy Lemon Yogurt Ice

Could an ice cream get cooler? I don't think so.

Directions

1. Grate the lemons and squeeze out all their juice. Discard the seeds. Mix in a large bowl.
2. Sift the sugar in. Stir to amalgamate. Rest for 30 minutes.
3. Tip the cream, yogurt, and water into another bowl. Whip together with a balloon whisk until just thick, not too stiff. Mix this gently into the lemon syrup with a metal spoon.
4. Pour the ice cream into a freezer container or freestanding freezer bag. Freeze. Get it out 10 minutes before you need it.

Serves 4
Ingredients
Juice of 6 large oranges
A good squeeze of lemon or lime juice

Orange Granita

A proper orange ice . . . so good . . . and totally refreshing.

Directions

1. Mix the orange juice and lemon or lime juice.
2. Pour it into a freezer bag or box. Set it in the freezer.
3. Every 20 to 30 minutes take it out. Break the ice up with a fork or whisk it.
4. Put it back in the freezer. Repeat another 4 times. Lasts 3 weeks.

Strawberry Sorbet

Homestyle strawberry slushie. Go pick your own fruit when strawberries are rampant. Refreshing for Verity after tennis.

Directions

1. Tip the sugar and water into a heavy-bottomed pan. Dissolve the sugar over low heat.
2. Increase heat and boil steadily for 5 minutes. Pour the syrup into a bowl. Add the lemon juice. Leave to cool.
3. Mash the strawberries into a liquid using a fork, or blitz. Add the syrup and blitz them together.
4. Pour the liquid sorbet into a freestanding freezer bag or container. Set it in the freezer until it starts to solidify. This could be 30 minutes or much longer, depending on your freezer.
5. Whisk the egg white. Take the solid sorbet out of the freezer and fold the egg white in to lift the mixture. Slap it back in the freezer.

Serves 4
Ingredients
1 cup sugar
2½ cups water
Juice of ½ lemon
12 ounces strawberries
1 egg white

Coconut Ice Cream & Lime Syrup

Great tastes, great team. Particularly soothing after curry or chili. The syrup works well on most fruit salads.

Directions

1. To make the ice cream by hand, tip the coconut milk into a bowl with the sugar and beat together. If using a blender, whisk the two together.
2. Pour the cream into a freezer bag or box. Slap it into the freezer.
3. Remove after 30 minutes. Break the mix up with a fork to reduce the ice crystals. Put it back in the freezer. Repeat.
4. When the ice cream starts to solidify, whisk the egg white till stiff. Fold it into the mix. Freeze again.
5. Tip the water and sugar into a heavy-bottomed pan over gentle heat. Stir with a wooden spoon to dissolve. Increase heat. Boil for 2 minutes.
6. Tip into a bowl. Cool. Add the lime zest and juice. Chill.
7. Drizzle the syrup over the ice cream.

Serves 4
Ingredients
Ice cream
1¾ cups coconut milk
½ cup sugar
1 egg white

Lime syrup
⅔ cup water
⅔ cup sugar
Finely grated zest and juice
  of 2 to 3 limes

Eat with:
Banana-filled crêpes
Banana sundae with
  chocolate sauce

Essential Extras

Real cooks have essential extras on hand.
So make 'em.

DOUGH

Short-crust Pastry

The real thing. Use it for all your pastry needs. Work fast with a light touch—you don't want concrete.

Makes 9-inch pie crust or 4 small tart pans

1¾ cups white flour
Pinch of salt
8 tablespoons butter
2 to 3 tablespoons very cold water

Directions

1. Sift the flour and salt into a large bowl. Cut the butter small.
2. Add the butter to the flour. Rub in lightly with your fingers till it looks like breadcrumbs.
3. Add 2 tablespoons of the cold water. Mix with a fork till the pastry starts to form. Bring the dough together quickly with your fingers. Handle very lightly. Add the remaining water if needed.
4. Wrap in plastic wrap and leave for 20 minutes to chill. Bring back to room temperature before using.

Processor method

1. Tip flour and salt into a processor.
2. Add butter. Process till mixed.
3. Add half the water. Process. Add the rest gradually (may not need it all) until pastry is soft and pliable, not sticky.
4. Remove on to a lightly floured board and use for recipe.

STOCKS

I freeze a lotta stock. Makes great soups, risotto, gravy, casseroles, and sauces.

Chicken Stock

1 roast chicken carcass
2 onions, quartered
1 celery stalk, cut into chunks
1 carrot, cut into chunks
Garlic cloves, peeled
1 leek, cut into chunks (optional)
A few fresh herb sprigs, tied with string (optional)
14 cups water

Directions

1. Chuck the chicken carcass with any fat, gravy, and meat into a large saucepan. Add the onions, celery, carrot, garlic, leek, and herbs (if using).
2. Pour in the water to cover. The pan should not be too full.
3. Bring to a boil. Skim off any scum. Simmer on a low heat for 2 to 3 hours.
4. Strain the stock through a colander over a large bowl. Cool. Cover with plastic wrap. Chill or freeze.

Vegetable Stock

2 large onions
1 celery stick
2 leeks
3 carrots
A few black peppercorns
Fresh parsley sprigs
10 cups water
Juice of 1 lemon
2 garlic cloves
2 teaspoons salt

Directions

1. Wash and roughly chop all the veg. Chuck into a large saucepan with all the other ingredients.
2. Bring to a boil. Cover partly. Simmer for 1 to 2 hours. Strain through a fine strainer.

DIPS, SAUCES, & SPREADS

Apple Chutney

Makes four 2-pound jars

4½-pounds cooking apples, peeled, cored, and chopped
4 cloves garlic, crushed
2½ cups malt vinegar
3 cups soft dark brown sugar
¾ cup chopped, pitted dates
3 teaspoons ground ginger
1 teaspoon allspice
1 teaspoon cinnamon
Large pinch of cayenne pepper
1 teaspoon salt

Directions

1. Tip the apples, garlic, and half the vinegar into a large heavy-bottomed saucepan.
2. Cook gently, stirring regularly with a wooden spoon till thick.
3. Add the remaining vinegar, sugar, dates, ginger, spices, and salt. Cook for 30 minutes, stirring, till thick and sludgy with the odd lump of fruit.
4. Wash jars well. Dry and place on a baking sheet. Warm in the oven at 275°F.
5. Ladle the chutney into the jars. Put a wax disk from a jam kit directly on to the chutney. Dampen a plastic-wrap disk to cover each pot. Secure with an elastic band.
6. Label and date when cold and replace the plastic wrap with lids. Leave for 2 months before eating.

Applesauce

2 apples, peeled, cored, and chopped
Blob of butter
Sugar
Squeeze of lemon juice
Ground cinnamon (optional)

Directions

1. Slap the apples in a pan with a bit of water and butter.

2. Cook very gently, stirring till the fruit gets mushy, adding more liquid if you need. Beat for a smooth sauce.

3. Taste and flavor with a bit of sugar and lemon juice and a pinch of ground cinnamon if you like.

Easy Raspberry Jam

Makes 6 small jars of jam
1 pound raspberries (fresh or defrosted)
1 pound sugar

Method
1. Sit your jars on a baking tray in a warm oven (275°F).
2. Put a plate in the fridge to chill.
3. Tip rinsed raspberries into a large heavy-bottomed pan. Cook gently for 2 to 3 minutes, stirring with a wooden spoon.
4. When the juices flow, add the sugar. Stir till it dissolves.
5. Whack up the heat and boil furiously for 5 minutes.
6. Do the set test. Get the plate from the fridge. Spoon a tiny bit of jam onto it. Leave for 1 minute, then push the jam with a finger. If it wrinkles up, then it is ready. If not, boil for a further 2 minutes then test again. Repeat till wrinkly.
7. Leave jam off the heat to settle for 5 minutes while you remove the warmed jars. Using a small ladle or large spoon, carefully fill each jar almost to the top. Take care; it will be so hot.

8. Top each pot with a disc of wax paper, wax side down. Then a transparent cover or lid. Wipe the jars down. Label and date when cool. Delicious.

Guacamole

2 shallots or 1 small onion, chopped
1 clove garlic, crushed
2 ripe avocados (Hass are good), peeled and pitted
Juice of 1 lemon or lime
Pinch of cayenne pepper
Pinch of salt
1 tablespoon fresh chopped cilantro (optional)

Homestyle Ketchup

1 pound (about four) ripe tomatoes (with stalks and stems attached), quartered
2 cloves garlic, crushed
1/3 cup brown sugar
4 tablespoons cider or white wine vinegar
Good pinch of mustard powder
4 shakes of Worcestershire sauce
Salt and pepper

Directions
1. Slap the ingredients into a large pan. Put on a medium-to-high heat and bring to a boil. Reduce at once. Simmer very gently for 45 to 60 minutes, or till the mix is sludgy with very little liquid.
2. Pull out any stems or stalks with a fork. Blitz the mix in a food processor or blender.
3. Pour through a strainer. Cool, then store in a sterilized jar (washed, then heated) or container. Can store in the fridge for two weeks.

Variation
At STEP 2, add 1 medium onion, quartered, and/or 1 fresh chili pepper.

Homestyle Mayo

2 egg yolks
1/2 teaspoon each of salt, dry mustard, and sugar
1 cup sunflower or peanut oil
1/4 cup olive oil

2 tablespoons white wine vinegar or lemon juice
1 tablespoon hot water

Directions
1. Beat the egg yolks, salt, mustard, and sugar in a bowl till smooth. Set the bowl on a tea towel to stop it from slipping.
2. Mix the oils in a pitcher. Pour the oil, drip by drip, onto the egg mix, whisking all the time. Keep it slow to start so that the mix won't curdle. After a bit it'll start to thicken.
3. When you've used half the oil, stop. Stir in 1 tablespoon vinegar or lemon juice.
4. Pour in the remaining oil in a slow trickle. Keep whisking.
5. Add the water and remianing vinegar or lemon.
5. Taste. Adjust the seasoning. Keeps for a week in an airtight container in the fridge.

Variations
At STEP 1, add for:
GARLIC MAYO (AIOLI)
2 crushed garlic cloves.

MUSTARD & DILL MAYO
2 teaspoons sugar and 2 tablespoons Dijon mustard. Then use 2/3 cup sunflower oil (no olive oil) and 1 tablespoon white wine vinegar. When mixed, stir in 1 to 2 tablespoons fresh chopped dill.

HOT MAYO
2 tablespoons wasabi or harissa paste instead of mustard.

Homestyle Pesto

1/4 pound fresh basil, cilantro, or arugula
2/3 cup olive oil
3 tablespoons pine nuts
2 large cloves garlic, peeled
1/2 cup grated Parmesan

Directions
1. Blitz everything but the cheese in a food processor.
2. Tip into a bowl. Mix in the Parmesan. Cover. Chill.

Hummus

15½-ounce can chickpeas, drained
2 cloves garlic, crushed
1 tablespoon tahini
Juice of 1 lemon
Pinch of salt
2 tablespoons olive oil
2 tablespoons water
Paprika (optional)
Fresh cilantro, chopped (optional)
A few pine nuts (optional)

Directions
1. Tip the chickpeas into a processor. Add the garlic, tahini, lemon juice, and salt.
2. Heat (don't boil) the olive oil and water in a small saucepan.
3. Add the liquid to the processor. Blitz till smooth. Add more water or lemon if the mix is too firm and blitz again.
4. Taste and season. Sprinkle with paprika, cilantro, and/or pine nuts.
5. Eat warm, or drizzle with olive oil and chill.

Tomato Salsa

4 ripe tomatoes, finely chopped
1 fresh red or green chili pepper, de-seeded and finely chopped
2 shallots or 1 small onion, finely chopped
2 tablespoons fresh chopped cilantro
1 lime
Pinch of sugar
Salt and pepper

Directions
1. Mix the tomatoes, chili pepper, shallots or onion, and cilantro.
2. Mix in a good squeeze or two of lime juice plus the sugar, salt, and pepper.

Tzatziki

1 cucumber, peeled and finely chopped
2 cloves garlic, crushed
1½ cups plain yogurt
Salt and pepper to taste

Directions
1. Mix the cucumber and garlic into the yogurt.
2. Season. Cover and chill.

Directions
1. Blitz the shallots or onion and garlic in a food processor.
2. Add the avocado flesh, lemon or lime juice, cayenne, salt, and cilantro (if using). Blitz again.
3. Cover and chill. Eat before it browns.

DRESSINGS & SALADS

Coleslaw

2 cups cabbage, shredded
1 large carrot, grated
1½ tablespoons mayo (page 139)
1 teaspoon mustard
Drizzle of honey
Handful of raisins or dates
Salt and pepper to taste

Directions
1. Stick the cabbage and carrot in a bowl.
2. Mix the other stuff.
3. Slap it over and mix well.

Green Salad

Any green leaves (e.g., arugula, butter-head, iceberg, watercress, romaine, baby spinach, chopped endive)

Directions
1. Mix any of these.
2. Toss in a simple olive-oil dressing or something creamy.

Honey & Mustard

2 teaspoons whole-grain mustard
1 teaspoon honey
1 clove garlic, crushed
2 tablespoons lemon juice or white wine vinegar
Salt and pepper to taste
6 tablespoons olive oil

Directions
1. Tip all the ingredients except the oil into a jar. Mix or shake.
2. Add the oil and mix again.

My Sparky Dressing

Good pinch of sugar
Pinch of salt

1 tablespoon balsamic vinegar
4 to 6 tablespoons extra-virgin olive oil

Directions
1. Whisk the sugar, salt, and vinegar together in a bowl. Add the olive oil bit by bit, or stick the lot in a jar, put the lid on, and shake it.
2. Taste and adjust the flavors.

Orange Salad

Green leaves: spinach, arugula, watercress, or chopped endive
2 oranges, peeled, sliced, and cut in segments (save juice)
2 carrots, grated
6 fresh dates or dried ones, chopped
Honey & Mustard dressing

Directions
1. Slap the leaves on two plates or bowls.
2. Top with the orange segments, carrots, and dates.
3. Toss with the dressing plus juice from the oranges.

Variation
Add cashew nuts or poppy seeds.

Orange & Pomegranate

2 oranges, peeled and sliced
Pomegranate molasses

Directions
Slap the oranges on a plate with a drizzle of pomegranate molasses for dipping. Fizzy.

Roast Pepper Salad

4 red or orange peppers
3 tablespoons olive oil
Salt and pepper to taste

Directions
1. Preheat oven to 450°F.
2. Set the peppers on a baking sheet. Cook for 30 minutes till blistered, turning once.
3. Set them in a freezer bag for 15 minutes, then peel and de-seed.
4. Cut into strips. Drizzle with the olive oil and season with salt and pepper.

Index

Tomato Salad

2 or 3 ripe tomatoes
A little salt and pepper
Pinch of caster sugar

Dressing

1 teaspoon sugar
1 teaspoon English or Dijon mustard
Salt and pepper
2 tablespoons wine vinegar (red,
    white, cider, sherry)
6 tablespoons olive oil
1 clove garlic, crushed (optional)

Directions

1. Slice the tomatoes into ⅓-inch
thick slices. Lay them on a plate in a
single layer. Sprinkle with the salt,
pepper, and sugar.

2. Whisk the dressing ingredients
together. Drizzle over the tomatoes
immediately to maximize the flavor.

3. Toss the tomatoes gently in the
dressing.

Variation

TOMATO & ONION SALAD

Chuck a finely chopped shallot or
thinly sliced red onion over dressed
tomato salad.

Zucchini Ribbon Salad

2 zucchini
2 tablespoons olive oil
1 tablespoon balsamic vinegar
1 clove garlic, crushed
Pinch of sugar
Salt and pepper to taste

Directions

1. Cut the ends off the zucchini.
Slicing lengthwise with a spud peeler,
make ribbons of very thin zucchini.
2. Whisk up the remaining
ingredients. Tip over the zucchini.

Index

Index

Cheers to Jess Taylor, Henry Preen, Ariyo Onafowokan, Joe Coulter, Andy Walkland, Olivia Towers, Verity Miers, and Dom Hanley for challenging me and being such great mates.

To York University, York City Football Club, and Next Generation Club for the use of their sports facilities; Imp-Hut Ltd. for the use of their recording studio; City Screen Ltd.; and the Farmer's Cart, Towthorpe.

To Louise Rooke (champion food taster and washer-up!).
To Dad for being Dad.
To Stevie G. for all the time off!
Thanks to Lorne and the Walker people.
Thanks to all my lovely family.
www.samstern.co.uk

Copyright © 2007 by Sam Stern and Susan Stern
Photography by Lorne Campbell
Susan Stern photograph by Jeffrey Stern

First U.S. edition 2009
Library of Congress Cataloging-in-Publication Data is available.
Library of Congress Catalog Card Number: 2008932510
ISBN 978-0-7636-3926-6

10 9 8 7 6 5 4 3 2 1

Printed in China

This book was typeset in GillSans.

Candlewick Press
99 Dover Street
Somerville, MA 02144
visit us at www.candlewick.com